RELEASE FROM
DEBTOR'S
PRISON

RELEASE FROM DEBTOR'S PRISON

ACHIEVING FINANCIAL FREEDOM

A PROVEN FORMULA FOR CHANGING THE ATTITUDES AND HABITS THAT KEEP YOU IN DEBT

MARGARET ST. JOHN

■ HAZELDEN®

INFORMATION & EDUCATIONAL SERVICES

Hazelden
Center City, Minnesota 55012-0176

1-800-328-0094
1-651-213-4590 (Fax)
www.hazelden.org

Library of Congress Cataloging-in-Publication Data

St. John, Margaret.
    Release from debtor's prison : achieving financial freedom : a proven
  formula for changing the attitudes and habits that keep you in debt /
  Margaret St. John.
      p.   cm.
    ISBN 1-56838-366-5
    1. Finance, Personal. 2. Debt. 3. Consumer credit. I. Title.
  HG179 .S55855 2000
  332.024—dc21   00-021891

Editor's note
The Twelve Steps and Twelve Traditions are reprinted and adapted with permission of Alcoholics Anonymous World Services, Inc. (AAWS). Permission
to adapt and reprint the Twelve Steps and Twelve Traditions does not mean
that AA has reviewed or approved the contents of this publication, or that AA
necessarily agrees with the views expressed herein. AA is a program of recovery from alcoholism *only*—use of the Twelve Steps and Twelve Traditions in
connection with programs and activities which are patterned after AA, but
which address other problems, or in any other non-AA context, does not
imply otherwise.
    The Twelve Steps, Twelve Traditions, and preamble of Debtors Anony-
mous are reprinted with permission of Debtors Anonymous World Services,
Inc. Permission to reprint this material does not mean that DA has reviewed
or approved the contents of this publication, or that DA necessarily agrees
with the views expressed herein.

Author's note
Although the names and identifying characteristics of the men and women
mentioned in this book have been changed to protect their anonymity, the
stories are real.
    In accordance with the principles of Twelve Step programs, the author has
protected her own anonymity by using a pen name.

04   03   02   01   00   6   5   4   3   2   1

Cover design by Theresa Gedig
Interior design by Donna Burch
Typesetting by Stanton Publication Services, Inc.

For my parents, who set my feet upon the path,
and
for all debtors everywhere who still suffer

Contents

1

"Financially Challenged"

I wouldn't say we're "broke."
I prefer to call it "financially challenged."
—cartoon caption

Drowning in bills marked "past due," the husband and wife in the cartoon caught my accountant's eye. She, more than anyone else, had had an inside track on the state of my finances for the previous five years. The year she enclosed the cartoon with my newly completed income tax returns for filing, I had just entered a recovery program most people had never heard of: Debtors Anonymous (DA). Although my accountant has never needed to walk through the door to a DA meeting herself, she has provided financial services to scores of people who desperately need what a financial recovery program has to offer. Debtors Anonymous, a fellowship of recovering debtors and money mismanagers, is a spiritual program based on the Twelve Steps of Alcoholics Anonymous.

Occasionally my above-and-beyond-the-call-of-duty accountant will give me a call to say, "I hope you don't mind, but I just shared your story, anonymously of course, with another beleaguered client." Of course I don't mind if my accountant wants to practice the Twelfth Step; that is, "to carry this message to compulsive debtors." I know, from my own experience, that compulsive debtors need all the help they can get. And if my financial life could be turned around, anybody's can.

"Financially challenged" is an accurate description of millions of Americans today. According to the United States Small Business Administration, total outstanding consumer installment debt rose above $1 trillion for the first time in 1995, and the Federal Reserve reports that American credit card debt, as of January 1999, amounted to $565.9 billion. In 1998, the total number of filings for bankruptcy in the United States was 1,442,549. According to the National Foundation for Consumer Credit, the average American family's outstanding unsecured debt, as of May 1999, was $6,000. The American Bankruptcy Institute reports that approximately 619 million checks were bounced in 1995, and that number is expected to jump to 731 million in the year 2000.

As a result of the dire circumstances of American consumers, the number of debt collection and credit reporting jobs is predicted to skyrocket to 2.93 million in 2005, an increase of 68.4 percent over 1994, when there were 1.74 million such jobs.

But, according to Mark Rosen, community relations manager at Consumer Credit Counseling Service of Michigan, the most distressing statistics are those reflecting personal savings trends in the United States. According to the Commerce Department, Americans were saving 2.9 percent of their income in 1996, 2.1 percent in 1997, and only .5 percent in 1998. But worse yet, as of March 1999, Americans were saving negative .6 percent; that is, they were withdrawing money from savings.

Undoubtedly, a variety of factors contribute to these alarming statistics, not the least of which is that, according to the National Foundation for Consumer Credit, three billion credit card solicitations were mailed out in 1998 and more than one billion credit cards are currently in use. The average family holds nine credit cards.

But, whatever the causes of the debt that millions of Americans have accrued, each person, each family, is accountable for its own share of that debt and its consequences. Not all those saddled with debt are out-of-control, habitual, compulsive debtors, but many are. The fact that our society is driven by the urge for immediate gratification and that consumerism is culturally sanctioned only aids and abets the problem.

But living in the problem will not change our debting patterns. Only living in the solution, as the Twelve Step programs say, can do that. We are lucky to live in a time in history when solutions are available, free for the taking. All that is required is willingness.

My "home" meeting (the meeting that you affiliate most consistently with) always concluded with a moment of silence for "the debtor who still suffers." I am eternally grateful that I no longer suffer from compulsive indebtedness. If sharing my story and the stories of others who are also recovering from this affliction can in any way relieve that suffering by opening the door to the transforming Steps, principles, and tools of Debtors Anonymous, then that is the least I can do. Again, as the Twelve Step fellowship always says, "You can't keep it unless you give it away." Writing these chapters has been another way of completing my Twelfth Step, which reads in full: "Having had a spiritual awakening as a result of these steps, we tried to carry this message to compulsive debtors and to practice these principles in all our affairs."

This book has been written for three types of readers. The first are those who have just discovered that they have a problem with indebtedness, that in fact they are more than "financially challenged." These readers may see themselves in some of the behaviors, attitudes, beliefs, and patterns that characterize compulsive debtors and may discover that there is a way out of their entrapment, just as there was for the recovering debtors mentioned in these pages.

The second group of readers are those who have already discovered Debtors Anonymous and are practicing the principles of the program but may be looking to explore more deeply the many levels of this debting dis-ease, the stuff that comes up after we've started to get our money in order. It is this group that may be particularly interested in discovering more about the many levels where debt hides in our lives, the continuous layers in which we find the debting state of mind causing pain and dysfunction.

Finally, I want to address readers who are concerned friends or family members, or helping professionals, who want to become better informed about a modern malaise that is becoming a virtual epidemic in American life.

To all readers, I offer the hope that the stories I tell may benefit them in the same way the stories of hundreds of debtors in scores of meetings have benefited me. The telling and hearing of our stories, so different, yet so similar, removes the isolation we feel when we remain silent.

Compulsive debting is an equal opportunity affliction; it includes people of both genders, from all ages, races, and socioeconomic groups. I have included a wide range of stories to represent this spectrum and have alternated the use of *he* and *she* to be as gender-inclusive as possible.

Back in the Black:
Escaping from Debtor's Prison

Be not made a beggar by banqueting upon borrowing.
— *Apocrypha Ecclesiasticus*

Six years ago on a winter's night I went to my first Debtors Anonymous meeting in New York City. I had run out of money completely—for the third time in my life. When it was my turn to "share" with the group, I simply said I was at the end of my financial rope and was planning on declaring bankruptcy, but I didn't know where I was going to get the money for an attorney. I had checked out three books from the library on do-it-yourself bankruptcy and was investigating the possibility of acting as my own counsel.

At the end of the meeting, eight people quietly came over to me, wanting to respond to my plight. "If you could just come to six meetings before you declare bankruptcy," one suggested, "you might see some other options. I've been where you are, and I can tell you that this is not about the money." The others concurred. I wanted to shout, "What do you mean it's not about the money? If I had some, I wouldn't be here."

Nevertheless, the quiet confidence of the man who had asked me to try out six meetings, and some of the comments I heard from other group members, together with my own sense of desperation and limited options, motivated me to return. I often wonder what would have happened if I had given in to my initial anger and skepticism and never returned. But, thankfully, I did come back for six meetings—which eventually became six years' worth of meetings that liberated me from the negative beliefs, attitudes, and behaviors that had kept me in debtor's prison for most of my life. In those early meetings I found myself undergoing a radical shift in attitude, a change in perspective that obliterated the long list of reasons I had enumerated as the cause of my financial woes. I thought I was in debt because I lived in a materialistic society, but I was not greedy; I thought I was in debt because I wasn't willing to sell my soul to do a job I didn't believe in, instead working in relatively low-paying service positions like high school teacher, book editor, freelance writer, and non-governmental organization administrator; I thought I was in debt because I was truthful whereas others cheated on their income tax; I thought I was in debt because I came from a family of ministers and religious educators who emphasized the value of spirituality; and I thought I was in debt because I was empathetic and other people did not care enough about the less fortunate.

But I myself was the source of my debt, because debting is the natural result of being a debtor—with debting beliefs, debting attitudes, and debting behaviors. Given what I believed and felt and did, the only place I could have been was in debt. And nothing was going to change until I changed. Only when this realization struck me with a sickening shock of recognition, only when I admitted my own responsibility for my circumstances and saw that the buck really did stop here, could I feel the hope that inevitably accompanies giving up being a victim of any set of circumstances: If I had caused it, although unconsciously, then I could make a decision to change it. I would not be able to change it by myself; my programming was too entrenched, my awareness too limited, and my need of other people and a Higher Power, fortunately, too human for me to go it alone.

During my first few months of attending DA meetings, I heard the program being characterized as the "Ph.D." of all Twelve Step programs. When I asked why, the answer I heard was that this was the most difficult, most painful of all the anonymous programs. It turned out that talking about money, and what money represented, was the most private and demanding of all topics. Drugs, alcohol, and sex seemed, from all reports, to be less threatening discussion topics than money. When I thought about it, I could see why. I had been involved in two anonymous programs before coming to DA. The Adult Children of Alcoholics (ACOA) fellowship existed to help men and women from alcoholic—or other dysfunctional backgrounds—deal with the long-term, debilitating effects of a chaotic family background. I had also participated in Al-Anon meetings, which focus on the attitudes of spouses or other enablers of alcoholics or drug addicts. I realized that DA was the most threatening program in my experience. While ACOA had been about family-of-origin issues and Al-Anon had been about current relationship and control issues, DA was closest to the bone: It was about my own sense of value and worth. I could not focus on anyone else; this raw issue was all mine.

Debtors Anonymous also seemed to include many variations on money-related issues and to affect many different levels and aspects of the lives of people attending the meetings. In other programs, all of the members used the same label to describe their addiction or orientation: "Hi, my name is . . . and I'm an alcoholic" or "adult child of an alcoholic." In DA I heard men and women introducing themselves with a wide range of labels: money mismanager, spendaholic, debtor, underearner, self-debtor, fantasy addict, compulsive spender. It seemed this program was the most complex of any I had been involved in or heard about. No wonder most Twelve Steppers came into this program last and called it their graduate program!

Throughout this book, I will describe the negative beliefs, attitudes, and behaviors that created debt or lack in numerous places in my life (including relationships, vocation, and the appropriate use of time and talents) and tell the story of how these negative orientations were gradually replaced by positive ones. I will demonstrate, with specific examples, how the Debtors Anonymous principles, tools, Steps, and meetings accomplished these changes in my life, as they can in yours.

Money and Our Personal History

I grew up in a tribe of ministers. My father, both my grandfathers, and all my uncles were pastors in either evangelical or mainstream Protestant denominations. For most of my childhood and adolescence, the boundaries of my world were formed by church-related friends, activities, and values.

The emphasis on spirituality and service that characterized my family and upbringing thankfully formed the foundation for my own lifelong values. Along with these values, however, came the traditional "baggage" that many people from such backgrounds carry. It was probably inevitable that I came to regard the material world, especially money itself, as an inferior order, almost in opposition to spiritual values. I was well acquainted with the Old Testament verse that says, "The love of money is the root of all evil" (often misquoted as "Money is the root of all evil") and the New Testament passage that states, "You cannot serve God and mammon." As a child, I did not know when passages were taken out of context or were "used" to support a particular viewpoint.

Misinterpretation of Scripture verses like "It is better to give than to receive" also led me to believe that the more I gave away and the less I had, the better. This type of thinking contributed to minimizing the importance of self-care in favor of taking care of others.

The air of secrecy that surrounded the topic of money in my family, like other families, also played a part in my conclusion that money was somewhat tainted. Early in my childhood I learned not to ask questions about financial matters, even if I could feel a crisis brewing. Such secrecy made me suspect that there was something shameful about money and that adults discussed it only when they couldn't avoid it any longer.

As a teenager I attended an academically prestigious high school in an affluent suburb of a large East Coast city. My classmates had fathers who made ten times the amount of money mine made. I could compete scholastically, but not in the social arena where money mattered. My girlfriends wore different cashmere sweaters every day of the week and received brand-new cars on their sixteenth birthdays. Although I acutely felt the difference in our living standards,

I kept telling myself that my family devoted its life to service, while the parents of my classmates were spending their lives making money.

Although my family never actively disparaged the need for money, I somehow got the idea that the less energy I spent thinking about it, the better off I would be. The stage was set for the way I would treat money for years to come— as if it were a necessary evil that I had to deal with to live in this world, but the less interaction I had with it, the better. I viewed money as irrelevant to anything important or worthwhile. Until the last six years, I never considered it when choosing a profession or when accepting a particular position. At some level, I behaved as if money did not exist.

For me, it is fascinating to look back on how I formed my beliefs about money. Each of us has created our own unique mythology about money that forms the basis of our present attitudes and behaviors, that causes us to relate to money in positive, creative ways or negative, destructive ways. Until we are aware of this set of beliefs, however, those of us with negative patterns in our financial lives are at the mercy of these unconscious attitudes. It was only when I hit my financial bottom that I was forced to confront my own negative mythology of money.

In a material world, living as if money does not exist is a recipe for disaster. It was only a matter of time until the faulty thinking that governed my choices would catch up to me. When it did, it took me quite a while to realize it. I was living in what is accurately called "denial." I was doing freelance writing and editing and kept thinking that something would rush in to save me—the big job, the big break. By the time reality broke through the wall of denial, I owed four years of back taxes to the Internal Revenue Service, was three months behind in my rent, was driving a broken-down car that had logged 143,000 miles, and had accrued thousands of dollars of debt to creditors as various as American Express, J.C. Penney, the local office supply store, and five personal friends.

I had stopped answering the phone and now screened every call to see if it was a creditor. I had already done the routine of promising irate bill collectors whatever they wanted, robbing one account to pay another in a vicious cycle that eventually ended in five accounts being turned over to collection agencies.

I no longer opened any envelope that resembled a bill; I couldn't pay anything anyway, so why open the mail? A large brown grocery bag in the closet stored all these un-opened communications. I found myself crossing the street in the business district of the town I lived in to avoid local creditors. I wrote out checks for three dollars' worth of gas to the Mobil station, hoping such a small amount would clear my bank account.

I walked into my first Debtors Anonymous meeting at this time. The fact that I had already hit bottom saved me a lot of time: I was too desperate to analyze or equivocate about the course of action I was counseled to follow. I had been earnestly listening to the stories of the people in these meetings and I wanted the same kind of transformation in my life that they had experienced in theirs. My plight gave me the most important attitude a newcomer to a Twelve Step program can have: willingness. I was ready to practice the principles of this program. The remaining pages of this chapter provide an overview of both the principles and the tools of the DA program. Chapters 3 through 10 will explore in greater detail how the principles and tools changed my life, and the lives of other DA members, in all the surprising places where debting attitudes and behaviors imprisoned us.

The Principles of the Debtors Anonymous Program as Found in the Twelve Steps

The following Steps have been adapted from Alcoholics Anonymous and are the basis of the Debtors Anonymous program.*

Admitting Powerlessness

Step One: We admitted we were powerless over debt—that our lives had become unmanageable.

By the time I walked into that first meeting, I had run out of money three different times in my life. I was beginning to understand that this situation was probably not an accident. Although I did not want to be in this situation, I was there. If I could have changed it, I would have, but clearly in the struggle between debt and me, debt kept winning. I admitted defeat, that I needed help, that my life was out of control, and that I could not put it back together by myself. Making this humbling admission in front of others immediately gave me an unpredictable sense of relief: I hadn't been able to allow myself to feel how tired I was, how exhausted from fighting a battle that I thought I should be

---

* The wording of the Twelve Steps has been adapted to speak directly to the reader. Adapted from the Twelve Steps of Alcoholics Anonymous with the permission of AA World Services, Inc., New York, N.Y. Reprinted with the permission of Debtors Anonymous World Services, Inc. (see editor's note on copyright page).

able to win. And every time I lost, I felt more humiliated—until the next time, when I would enter the battle again, this time with even more determination to win.

As soon as I admitted my powerlessness over debt, this struggle immediately ceased. My unrealistic, egotistic expectations of myself—that I should know how to do something that I didn't know how to do—gave way to acknowledging that I needed, and was ready to accept, help. Asking for help was a big step for me; I was used to giving help, not asking for it. In accepting what I was powerless over, I also learned what I was powerful over, what I had choices about, what was properly in my control. I realized that the decision to ask for help was a choice I was powerful over. Being able to distinguish between what was in my control and what was not was a big step in living in accordance with reality, a skill I had not developed very well.

The energy I had expended on fighting debt—a struggle that didn't hurt debt at all but wore me out—was now available to simply follow the principles of the program, principles that would change me so that debt would, over time, simply disappear, without a fight, from my life.

Acknowledging Insane Behavior with Money

Step Two: Came to believe that a Power greater than ourselves could restore us to sanity.

As I often heard people say in meetings, the reason this Step is so difficult is that it directly implies that they have been insane, and no one wants to admit this. It was very clear to me, however, that my behavior with money had been insane and that I myself was incapable of remedying the situation. Anyone in his or her right mind would not have run out of money three times in the matter of forty-some years. As the common definition goes, insanity is doing the same thing over and over while expecting a different result. In program terminology, this type of behavior is attributed to "stinking thinking." I realized that my attitudes in the area of money fell into the category of "insane" and that only intervention from a source outside myself could change them.

Trusting an All-Wise Power

Step Three: Made a decision to turn our will and our lives over to the care of God as we understood Him.*

For forty-some years I had tried to run my money affairs by myself—with nothing but failure and near-bankruptcy as a result. I knew I was not managing my life very well, so I was willing to turn my life over to a benign source, but my problem with this Step was around trust. I realized I wasn't sure God had my best interests at heart; I wasn't sure I could entrust the outcome of my life to him or her. By the time I arrived at this Step, though, I had been to enough meetings and heard enough stories to know that people who had taken this Step had not had their trust abused. With the support of other people whose stories I believed and identified with, I did make the decision to let go of relying on my own fallible resources and to ask an all-wise Power to take charge.

Making a List of Character Traits

Step Four: Made a searching and fearless moral inventory of ourselves.

This Step required that I write out a list of the attitudes

---

* The Twelve Steps use the masculine pronoun for God, but many people in Twelve Step meetings use *Her* instead of or interchangeably with *Him*.

and personal qualities that had landed me in my debtor's prison. This list was in no way meant to affix blame; it had the same purpose as an actual business inventory. I was simply taking stock of my character traits so I could benefit from seeing how I had arrived at financial collapse. This Step was like shining a flashlight into a dark stockroom to see what was on the shelves. Next to the column of personal qualities I listed the results of each of these character traits. What had each quality brought about in my life? How had it specifically affected me? What was the result of having a particular attitude? For example, my attitude of entitlement—the belief that people with more money somehow "owed" me—caused resentment within me while creating ill will in my relationships.

Confessing Our Shortcomings

Step Five: Admitted to God, to ourselves, and to another human being the exact nature of our wrongs.

An old adage says, "Confession is good for the soul." Until we actually admit our shortcomings to our Higher Power and another human being, they are not fully real. It is easy to play games with ourselves and to escape from taking full responsibility for the results of our attitudes and actions, but when we read our list aloud, we hear ourselves claim our own role in our financial situation and get acknowledgment and support for moving beyond our current situation.

Letting Go

Step Six: Were entirely ready to have God remove all these defects of character.

We cannot be ready to have our negative attitudes and

flaws removed until we know what they are and are ready to change. Steps Four and Five prepare us for this Step. The Step says that all we have to do is be ready for our defects to be removed; we don't have to use willpower or force or wage a war against ourselves. We simply have to be willing to let go.

Acknowledging Our Shortcomings

Step Seven: Humbly asked Him to remove our shortcomings.

The word that always seems most prominent in this Step is *humbly*. Before most debtors I know came into DA, they were still operating with the belief that they could successfully run their own lives—regardless of proof to the contrary. Having humility means acknowledging our limitations; it prepares us to ask for the removal of our shortcomings identified in Step Four.

Making a List of Creditors

Step Eight: Made a list of all persons we had harmed and became willing to make amends to them all.

In other programs, this list is usually made up of friends, family members, and colleagues. In Debtors Anonymous, however, it is usually a list of our creditors, those we have harmed by not keeping our agreement to pay for goods and services we have already received. My list included the Internal Revenue Service, credit card companies, a bank, department stores, shops in my hometown, and personal friends. Next to each name I wrote the amount I owed.

Contacting Creditors

Step Nine: Made direct amends to such people wherever possible, except when to do so would injure them or others.

In Debtors Anonymous, this Step usually means making direct contact with each creditor to clarify the status of our debt and to indicate our intention of paying the debt in full, according to a realistic payment plan. Many debtors new to the program are unable to meet their monthly payments and are in arrears. They may be paying a portion of the balance due or they may be unable to pay anything. Usually they are juggling accounts and promising to pay unrealistic amounts, creating further ill will with their creditors. More on dealing with creditors follows later in this chapter.

Making Progress

Step Ten: Continued to take personal inventory and when we were wrong, promptly admitted it.

Working this program is a process; the Steps are not taken once and for all. As one of the mottoes of the Twelve Step programs says, the goal is progress, not perfection. Continuously taking inventory of our attitudes and personal qualities means we are always on the journey, never fully arriving. This path is not a linear one, with a straight line beginning at point A and ending at point Z. It is more like a spiral; we are continuously moving along our path but the same issues may show up at even deeper levels as the succeeding chapters in this book will show, bringing us more maturity and preparing us for the next challenge in our lives.

Cultivating Spiritual Practices

Step Eleven: Sought through prayer and meditation to improve our conscious contact with God as we understood Him, praying only for knowledge of His will for us and the power to carry that out.

As a spiritual program, Debtors Anonymous is rooted in the belief in a Higher Power or, as the Twelve Step programs say, the "God of our understanding." Each person in the program comes to his or her own belief about who or what the Higher Power is. For many people, their Higher Power is the God of their particular religious faith; other people say their Higher Power is found in the love and compassion that emerges from their particular Twelve Step group. Whatever constitutes the Higher Power, though, a belief in something larger than oneself is at the core of the Twelve Step programs, and maintaining contact with that Power through a spiritual practice is essential to practicing the principles of Debtors Anonymous. My own practice centers around a time of daily meditation using what the Christian tradition calls "centering prayer," as well as at least one daily reading from a spiritual book.

Giving It Away

Step Twelve: Having had a spiritual awakening as a result of these Steps, we tried to carry this message to compulsive debtors and to practice these principles in all our affairs.

During my first few months in DA, I kept hearing about the importance of service. "You can't keep it unless you give it away," people at meetings said. I did do service work in very small ways when I first became involved in the program, but it was a while before I had enough experience, strength, and hope of my own to share my story and to render service, like sponsoring people new to the program, serving on pressure groups, and leading meetings.

I began to spend time on a regular basis each week working with compulsive debtors who were just starting to keep a spending record, who needed to check in by telephone when they felt a spending fit coming on, or who wanted to "bookend" (defined as making a phone call to a DA buddy before and after taking a DA action Step) a phone call to a creditor they feared. Later, after I had more experience using the DA tools, I began to serve on pressure groups (to be discussed later in this chapter) and to act as a sponsor. Just as I had been told, I found that I received just as much as I gave. To be able to share the benefits I had been given not only helped debtors as desperate as I had been, but also furthered my own recovery. The bonds that formed between my sponsorees and me and the growth that came through honestly sharing our secrets and our shame around our money issues established a trust and intimacy that we treasure to this day.

The principles of the program, epitomized in the Steps, are the basis of the Debtors Anonymous program. They changed my relationship to money. But the tools of DA, used on a regular basis, also transformed my financial life. More than any other Twelve Step program, DA is considered to be a program of action steps. A friend of mine once observed that there are more concrete actions, such as keeping a spending record and implementing a spending plan, for recovering debtors than other addicts because becoming solvent involves both a substance (money) and a process (the exchange of money in daily transactions). Unlike Alcoholics Anonymous, which deals with a substance, alcohol, and Codependents Anonymous, which deals with relationships, not with a substance, debtors must deal with both the substance of money and interactions using money for the rest of their lives. It is not possible to abstain from money or to break off a relationship with it. It is a permanent part of our lives and if we do not manage it, it will truly make our lives unmanageable.

Selected Tools of the Debtors Anonymous Program*

1. Meetings

Just as alcoholics stay sober by not drinking one day at a time, so debtors become solvent by not debting one day at a time. Because not spending compulsively, not charging, and not borrowing are so difficult for the newly recovering debtor, the concept of one day at a time is crucial to recovery. The most important tool for supporting solvency one day at a time is attendance at meetings. At least one meeting a week is recommended for newcomers. I attended two meetings a week for the first couple of years and subsequently went to one group per week. Programs that address substance abuse suggest that newcomers go to ninety meetings in ninety days as a way of reinforcing the transition from an addictive lifestyle to a sober one. This may be difficult for debtors, however, since there are currently far fewer DA meetings throughout the United States than there are Alcoholics Anonymous or Narcotics Anonymous meetings.

Meetings vary in emphasis and in participants. In large

---

* Throughout this book, the author has chosen certain tools of Debtors Anonymous for her discussion. She has numbered these tools in a way that reflects her prioritization. However, Debtors Anonymous has twelve official tools that it uses in its meetings, and they are priortized in the following way: abstinence, meetings, record maintenance, anonymity, the telephone, pressure relief groups and pressure relief meetings, spending plans, sponsor, business meetings, AA and DA literature, awareness, and service. For more information about Debtors Anonymous, please refer to appendixes B, D, and E or contact their world service office at P.O. Box 920888, Needham, MA 02492-0009, (781) 453-2743, or visit their Web site at www.debtorsanonymous.org

metropolitan areas the choices are greater, but all you need to get financially sober is one meeting. *Speaker meetings* offer the opportunity to hear one person tell her story for about twenty or thirty minutes and then open the meeting for other people to share. *Topic meetings* focus on a theme of common concern—charging, bill collectors, compulsive spending, right livelihood. *Step meetings* discuss the application of one of the Twelve Steps to the problem of compulsive indebtedness. I usually tried a new meeting several times before deciding whether to make it a regular part of my recovery program.

Although approximately one hundred different DA groups meet weekly in the greater New York City area, not all cities or areas have such a large support system with so many meeting choices. Meetings include such a wide variety of titles as "Sunday Afternoon Steps," "Right Livelihood," "Visions," "Prosperity," "Business Owners Debtors Anonymous," "Undercarners Step Clinic," and "Abundance Unlimited." When I moved outside New York, I found only one meeting in my new area, but one meeting was enough to support me in practicing the principles of the program.

Meetings are important for the support they offer in working the Steps and using the tools, but they are also important because they are the context in which debtors tell and retell their stories, gaining insight and perspective on their lives in the telling and the hearing of these stories. In the presence of others who share the same money malady, the individual stories become part of a larger, commonly shared story that releases the participants from their bondage of isolation and, over time, transforms the troubled relationships with money into sane relationships that work.

2. The Spending Record

I have written down every penny I have spent for the last six years, with the exception of one month a couple of years ago when I was taking care of a terminally ill parent. This basic tool is one of the most important in the Debtors Anonymous program because it brings the debtor out of vagueness and into reality. Most debtors have no idea whatsoever where their money goes. It just vanishes. This tool, faithfully used, tells the debtor exactly where every penny goes. I keep my money record in my day-at-a-glance book so I can never misplace the figures, but some people write their figures down on slips of paper or in a small notebook and transfer them to spreadsheets later.

At the end of each week, the figures are recorded in categories (see the example from my own numbers records at the conclusion of chapter 5, page 99). Then, at the end of the month, the weekly totals are added up to arrive at a monthly figure for each category. The monthly record shows exactly where the money has gone, and it is usually a big surprise. For example, I was astounded, reviewing my first monthly record, to see that I had spent thirty dollars on coffee from take-out shops! I had no idea I was spending that much money on coffee. The numbers never lie; they paint an accurate picture of one's life. Any lopsided values, any areas where needs are not being met, areas where extravagance rules—all show up in the numbers. Once we find out where the money goes, we see why we hid our expenditures from ourselves. Unawareness covers a multitude of sins.

The spending record provides us with the opportunity not only to see where the money has gone, but also to learn to make reality-based choices. Do we really want to spend our money this way? This invaluable tool is the beginning of conscious decision-making and appropriate control over our spending patterns; it allows us to make choices about our expenditures with awareness. The spending record can be started anytime. It is not necessary to start it at the beginning of the month. The important part is to keep a consistent record of your spending for at least sixty days.

3. The Spending Plan

In my experience, most spending plans are created with the help of a pressure group. Usually two months or so of spending records are brought to the two people serving as the pressure group. These two people (ideally a man and a woman), who have experience in the program, go through the records with the debtor, looking for categories that may indicate an imbalance in the record-keeper's life. A record may indicate, for example, that so much money is being spent on a sports car that there are insufficient funds available for personal care or household appliances. Sometimes categories are completely missing. For example, I had no clothing allowance in my records, yet I worked a professional job that demanded appropriate attire. I didn't even notice this omission until my pressure group pointed it out.

Once the appropriate categories for a spending plan are determined, a reasonable figure, often based on the reality of the spending records, is allocated to each category. The basic rule governing the plan is a simple one: expenditures cannot exceed income. If, according to the spending records, expenditures do exceed income, then there are three choices: increase the income, decrease the expenditures, or work out a plan that combines both. If an adjustment is not made, then debting will be the inevitable result, and debtors cannot get out of debt by debting.

After a spending plan has been created, then the implementation begins. It can always be adjusted as it is tested over time. It's best to keep spending records on the same spreadsheet as the spending plan so that weekly totals can be compared with the plan's monthly allocation for each category. Although all this paperwork may seem daunting at first, the freedom and control it provides the record-keeper more than makes up for any inconvenience or drudgery. An actual plan and record from one of my own spreadsheets serves as an example at the end of chapter 7 (pages 144–45).

After totaling the weekly records for the month, the recordkeeper compares that total to the amount in the spending plan. The last column on the sheet, labeled "+ or -," lets the record-keeper know whether she has exceeded the amount in the plan and, if so, by how much. Again, see the end of chapter 7.

The spending plan/spending record tool is invaluable in staying out of vagueness and in reality with one's money. When it is kept on a regular basis, it will give any money mismanager the ability to make choices based on the reality of his situation and bring balance and order to his financial life.

4. Pressure Meetings

The purpose of the pressure meeting is to provide relief from the pressure of the situation the debtor is in. Usually a list of action steps that will help relieve the pressure is created by the end of the meeting. When followed, these steps will usually alleviate a great deal of the stress surrounding whatever issue has been paramount for the debtor.

A pressure meeting is composed of three people: the person who requests the meeting, and a man and a woman whose experience, strength, and hope have been particularly helpful in meetings. Often the pressure group meets to review spending records and create a spending plan, but it may meet for a variety of other reasons: to create a debt repayment plan, to work on issues of right livelihood, or to review action steps from a previous pressure group meeting.

5. The Debt Repayment Plan

Most debtors come into the program saddled with debts. They may barely be meeting their monthly payments, or perhaps they are unable to meet payments at all. In my case, several debts had already been turned over to collection agencies by the time I arrived in Debtors Anonymous.

Usually the spending records and spending plan will reveal whether there is adequate money available to meet the debtor's needs and also repay the accumulated debts. If no money is available for debt repayment, then a request-for-a-debt-moratorium plan is put in place. Debtors write a letter to each creditor (usually obtaining the name of an individual they can continue to communicate with), stating their intention to repay the full amount of the debt and asking for a ninety-day moratorium on payments. This moratorium gives debtors a cushion of time to continue to work with their pressure group to develop a realistic plan that can actually be implemented.

Often within that ninety-day period the spending plan can be refined to include at least a small sum of money that can be allocated to debt repayment. Even if the total amount of money available for debt repayment is only one hundred dollars, at least a realistic beginning can be made to repay creditors. A percentage system is used to ensure fairness to all creditors. For example, if the amount owed to a particular credit card company is one-half of the entire debt load, and the amount of money available for repayment is one hundred dollars, then that credit card company would receive fifty percent of one hundred dollars, or fifty dollars.

At the end of the ninety-day moratorium, the debtor makes sure he contacts each creditor as promised, specifying the amount of money he can pay on a monthly basis and sending the first check—even if it is only three dollars. Once the company has cashed the check, it has tacitly agreed to the repayment plan. Although some debtors do run into difficulty with creditors trying to implement their repayment plan, I myself, as well as the majority of people I know, have been able to repay the majority of their debt using this time-tested system.

6. The Telephone Support System

Although this tool may seem trivial in comparison to the very specific tools already discussed, it cannot be underestimated. Most Debtors Anonymous groups have phone lists of members, and attendees may copy down the names and phone numbers of people whose comments have been helpful to them during meetings. Using the telephone to check in with other people keeps recovering debtors working their program. The phone can be used to check in weekly numbers (defined as the totals at the end of every week of the spending record), to report the balancing of a checkbook, to discuss the validity of a proposed purchase, or to bookend a difficult action step, such as contacting a creditor or cutting up a credit card.

7. Sponsorship

This tool is found in every Twelve Step fellowship and it is one of the most important aspects of working an anonymous program. A sponsor provides guidance to sponsorees to grow in the program—by supporting them in working the Steps and being available for check-ins at least weekly on the phone or in person. A deep bond usually develops between the sponsor and the sponsoree that provides mutual growth and encouragement on the Twelve Step journey. These relationships are often long-lasting and even transcend geographical distance. I have found sponsorship to be one of the most beneficial tools in my own personal growth in Debtors Anonymous. Giving away what we have found enlarges our capacity to receive even more!

Although money is only the tip of the iceberg when it comes to recovery from compulsive indebtedness, without addressing money concerns first, debtors would not be able to proceed to deal with the deeper issues money represents. It is these issues, where painful self-debting behaviors and feelings of worthlessness live, that hibernate beneath our money malaise.

The Twelve Steps of Debtors Anonymous

1. We admitted we were powerless over debt—that our lives had become unmanageable.

2. Came to believe that a Power greater than ourselves could restore us to sanity.

3. Made a decision to turn our will and our lives over to the care of God as we understood Him.

4. Made a searching and fearless moral inventory of ourselves.

5. Admitted to God, to ourselves, and to another human being the exact nature of our wrongs.

6. Were entirely ready to have God remove all these defects of character.

7. Humbly asked Him to remove our shortcomings.

8. Made a list of all persons we had harmed, and became willing to make amends to them all.

9. Made direct amends to such people wherever possible, except when to do so would injure them or others.

10. Continued to take personal inventory and when we were wrong promptly admitted it.

11. Sought through prayer and meditation to improve our conscious contact with God as we understood Him, praying only for knowledge of His will for us and the power to carry that out.

12. Having had a spiritual awakening as a result of these Steps, we tried to carry this message to compulsive debtors, and to practice these principles in all our affairs.

How Did I Get into This Mess?
Identifying the Roots
of Our Indebtedness

Melanie: What I can't figure out is,
how did things turn out like this?
Sponsor: When I hear your story, I think,
how could they have turned out any other way?

The Thursday night Debtors Anonymous meeting was
packed. The third Thursday of the month was usually a
speaker's meeting, and tonight Susan was telling her story.
Unlike Step meetings, which focus on one of the Twelve
Steps, or topic meetings, which center on a topic like resentment or credit card debt, a speaker meeting offers the
DA group an opportunity to hear a member tell his story,
his personal history with money and indebtedness.

A petite, attractive blond in her mid-forties, Susan was
always impeccably dressed. Tonight was no exception. Her
crisp white linen suit and Ferragamo pumps were accented
by a red Coach handbag, and her French manicure drew attention to a costly diamond and emerald wedding ring.

"I grew up in a very status-conscious town in Westchester

County," Susan began. "Where you lived, what kind of car you drove, whether you wore the right designer clothing were all very important and became for me a measure of worth. Most of the time I managed to look like I belonged in the set I ran with, but it was tough because my father was not only supporting our family of five, but also contributing to the support of his younger brother and sister.

"Then, when I was sixteen, disaster struck. One April afternoon Mom got a call from the accounting firm where Dad was a CPA saying he'd been rushed to the emergency room with a heart attack. From then on, life was one medical crisis after another. A series of strokes brought Dad closer and closer to complete paralysis, and he died two years later.

"I don't know what kind of medical insurance my parents had, but what I do know is that the sizable savings Mom and Dad had were completely eaten up by the medical bills. There was nothing left. I had to work my way through college and then, when I married, I worked two jobs while my husband was in law school. I scrimped and saved and cooked rice and beans and stretched every dollar to the max.

"When my husband finally graduated from law school and joined a firm, I got my first credit card. I also started my own business and today I am a successful antiques dealer. But as soon as I got that first credit card, I began charging, and pretty soon I was completely out of control. I charged not only things for my business but also for my home. And then I began compulsively buying clothes, jewelry, and accessories for myself. It had been so long since I'd had anything beautiful that I felt I deserved to treat myself. I guess I felt like I was a famine victim and now it was time to feast.

"But the spending just took over. It had a life of its own, and I just couldn't stop charging. I had to get another card, and then another, because I was over my limit. I told myself I could get this situation under control because my husband was making good money, I was making good money, and we had no dependents. But somehow the charge card balances kept spiraling upward, and my life began spiraling downward. My need to spend was so great that I couldn't even go home after closing up my shop without charging something first. It was my little adrenaline high for the day.

"One day my husband opened my Visa bill by mistake and couldn't believe his eyes. By the time the smoke cleared, I had had to acknowledge, to myself and to him, that I had incurred $86,000 worth of credit card debt. Admitting my spendaholic behavior felt humiliating, but some sane part of me was secretly relieved to have this roller-coaster ride come to an end.

"Since coming into Debtors Anonymous two years ago and applying the principles of this program to my situation, I have paid off $30,000 of my credit card debt. But even more important, I have not incurred any new debt since the day I sought help. I will probably always have a spendaholic streak in me, but today I know I have choices and that I can get support to live my life from a healthier attitude."

> If you always do what you always did,
> you'll always get
> what you always got.
> —Anonymous

Like so many other addictions and compulsions, compulsive debting has its roots in our personal past, in our experience of growing up in our particular family of origin. When we start to unravel the cord of our own history with money, we will inevitably uncover the source of our own behaviors, attitudes, and beliefs around a substance perceived to be so powerful that men and women have killed each other to obtain it and jumped from skyscrapers in the thirties as a result of losing it.

And, like other addictions and compulsions, compulsive debting and/or money mismanagement tends to be a family affliction, often showing up across generations and wreaking emotional and financial havoc until someone short-circuits the family pattern by going for help and breaking the indebtedness cycle.

A Clue—How We Treat Money

Our life story reveals everything we need to know. We just need to pay attention. Whatever our dis-ease with money might be—overspending, underearning, charging, loaning—the seeds of the cure can be found within the disease itself. How we treat our money, how we manage our finances, is just a clue, a picture, of how we regard our resources, of what we value, of where we place our energy, of what we think we are worth. The distortions in our financial life are simply pointing out unhealthy patterns that are not serving us, patterns asking to be cleared so that we can "put our money where our mouth is," so that our relationship with money can reflect the values we say we believe in, so that there is coherence between where our money goes and where our life is going, so that we can exercise choices about our finances instead of being victimized by them.

Why Compulsive Debting Becomes a Prison

Merriam Webster's Collegiate Dictionary defines *debt* as "a state of owing" and a *debtor* as "one guilty of neglect or violation of duty." Most debtors I have encountered are able to enumerate what sound like logical reasons for their financial condition. But these reasons don't change the fact that they live inside a "state of owing." The word *state* implies a condition or a way of being, and indeed, compulsive debting does become a way of life, a trap, a prison. When we debt, we are trying to get something we need or want, but we are not participating in an immediate, equal exchange between the supplier of goods and services and us, the purchasers. Instead, we obtain the commodity and postpone the payment, thus living in a state of owing and becoming guilty of neglect.

Sadly, many compulsive debtors end up forfeiting a sense of their own worth and value to obtain things they desire, for one cannot remain inside a state of owing without eventually living out of a sense of obligation and deprivation. No punishment needs to be meted out to a compulsive debtor. Living from lack, from obligation, from a state of owing is punishment enough. It may take years for our debt to catch up with us, and we may be accomplished at deluding ourselves, but for compulsive debtors, in the end debt will get the upper hand.

A Treasure Hunt

When we review our personal history and begin to tell the story of our relationship to money, we start to uncover our own financial mythology. We become aware for the first time that we have a story that can tell us everything we need to know about our attitudes toward, feelings about, and beliefs regarding money. By studying the plotline of our personal story, the history of our behavior with money, we make our mythology conscious and start to see it as an entity outside ourselves that can give us vital, valuable information about how we got into the mess we're in and some clues about how we can get out. This journey into the past in order to clearly see the present and change the future is like a treasure hunt.

The treasure we will discover is the exciting opportunity to write a new script for our money story, beginning now. Money is a symbol of our life energy. We give our time, talents, and experience to our work, and we are compensated in the form of money. Our earnings represent the energy we have expended in our job. How we handle these earnings, or any money that comes to us, is a picture of how we are handling our life's energy. The way we deal with money is a picture of the way we deal with life: we can squander it, hoard it, give it away, save it, invest it, spend it wisely, loan it, lose it.

Poverty—A Lack of Options

People possessing great wealth often wield considerable power and influence in their communities, their businesses, and their social situations. Their money is perceived as an *empowering* force. For compulsive debtors, however, living in a state of owing is enervating, not empowering. I once heard someone in a DA meeting characterize poverty as "a lack of options." Not managing our life's energy in appropriate, healthy ways does reduce our options and depletes us, leaving us no resources either in the bank or in our personal lives.

When we tell our story, it begins to have an identity outside of us and we gain some distance and perspective on it. Our story no longer owns or possesses us; we hear the stories of others and see new possibilities. We see our story more clearly, but we realize that this isn't the only story there is about how to have a relationship with money. We begin to have access to new possibilities, new stories.

Peeling the Onion

In exploring our story, in mining it to gain awareness and insight, we start by looking at our *behavior* toward money. The behavior is significant, but it is only the tip of the proverbial iceberg. Underneath our behavior, at the next level of our money mythology, are our attitudes and feelings about money. And finally, the deepest level of our mythology is our belief system about money. We have little or no awareness of our belief system. The more we can learn about it, the more we will see the connection between our most deeply held convictions and our financial situation.

Using Susan's story (from the DA speaker meeting) as our laboratory for exploration, let's unravel her plotline. We can look at it as an onion that is being peeled layer by layer. We see that she grew up in a fairly affluent suburb where material possessions were important as status symbols and indicators of worth and where she had to make an effort to belong. Her nuclear family had financial obligations to the extended family, siphoning off resources from Susan and her siblings. Then she experienced further loss of resources because of a family medical disaster that wiped out all savings. Susan then had to pay her own way to college *and* worked two jobs while her husband was in school.

Between the ages of sixteen and twenty-five, Susan experienced some fairly steady financial hardship. Then, at age twenty-six, she got her first credit card and at age twenty-eight opened her own business. She began charging. This habit escalated as she made more money and finally became a compulsion, creating $86,000 of credit card debt. These behaviors landed Susan in debtor's prison and finally in Debtors Anonymous.

But what were the attitudes and feelings underneath these behaviors? What emotional components lived in the next level of Susan's mythology of money? As a young teenager surrounded by affluence, Susan felt somewhat "less than" her friends, who came from more affluent homes. Then when disaster struck, she felt she could not compete with the in-group at all, and she went into survival mode, adopting a stance of hardy independence and autonomy, all the while feeling deprived for having to work so hard for what her friends had received through the circumstances of their birth. She chose to work hard, but her feeling was of having to grit her teeth, bite the bullet, pull herself up by her own bootstraps. When she and her husband finally made it over the education hump and began earning good money, Susan, exhausted and short on luxuries, felt she deserved a reward for her years of hardship. Her attitude included a characteristic of most debtors—entitlement. "I deserve it; I have it coming to me."

What deeply held beliefs unconsciously ruled Susan's choices about money matters? Her early years had instilled the belief that you are what you have and that she was never quite enough because she never had quite enough. But the most pervasive and controlling belief, the one that really got

Susan in trouble with credit cards, was this: "I better get what I want right now because if I don't some disaster will come along to use it up anyway." There was a sense of urgency in Susan's spending, a belief that you have to get it while you can.

DA Meetings—The First Tool

Just like Susan, most of us do not know what is driving our behavior around money. Even if we did know what this force was, there is no guarantee we could stop it by ourselves. Awareness is the beginning of change and is usually a prerequisite for change, but by itself it does not guarantee new beliefs, attitudes, and behaviors. That is why compulsive debtors are fortunate to have a Twelve Step program all their own. Debtors Anonymous offers the same kind of relief from compulsive indebtedness that Alcoholics Anonymous provides to men and women suffering from alcoholism. When we have a safe place to take our stories, to share our dis-ease around money, to practice the Twelve Steps and the tools, then we are enabled to see where we have been and to start changing the direction in which we are going.

The Importance of Fellowship

Debtors Anonymous is a fellowship of men and women
who share their experience, strength and hope
with each other that they may solve their common problem
and help others recover from compulsive debting.
—Debtors Anonymous Preamble

For most people who recover from compulsive indebtedness through the Debtors Anonymous program, the DA meetings are the first program tool they encounter. That was certainly my experience, and without attendance at the meetings, I could not have learned how to live in sobriety with my money—no matter how many spending records I kept, how many spending plans I made, or how many repayment plans I implemented.

It was coming into the human circle, encountering other real people from all walks of life who were also suffering from the effects of intemperance with money, that first gave me hope when I had none, provided alternatives when I saw none, and told me I was not alone when I was feeling as if I were the only person in the world who had months' worth of unopened bills in a grocery bag in the closet. As I listened to the spontaneous, unself-conscious sharing that took place in "the rooms," I began to feel that there might be a shred of hope in the midst of financial despair—even for me.

The first thing the powerful tool of attendance at meetings did for me was break my isolation, my secrecy, the sense that I was alone with this problem and I better not talk about it because then everyone would know how unskilled I was with money management. In meetings I was at first taken aback and then relieved to hear men and women openly sharing their mishaps with credit cards, the IRS, and bank loans. The more meetings I attended, the more I felt I had rejoined the human race.

Putting a Name on It

The second gift that meetings gave me was to break my denial about my situation. I certainly knew when I came to my first meeting that I was in deep trouble—with the IRS, four major credit card companies, local business owners, and friends. But I did not know that I was suffering from compulsive indebtedness, that there were causes of this condition, and that there was a cure for it. Before my first meeting, I had never said to anyone, including myself, "I am a debtor." To say that would have been humiliating and increased the annihilating shame I already felt. But seeing men and women of all ages, backgrounds, and socioeconomic groups openly admit their indebtedness and still be able to hold their heads up allowed me to move from humiliation to humility.

Admitting

I was a debtor and accepting the fact of my debt was surprisingly freeing. Only in the human circle, in a meeting, could the admission "I am a debtor" be transforming. "Getting real" by naming my situation out loud in the presence of other people allowed me to admit my debt, accept it, and move on. I no longer wasted energy concealing from myself and everyone else the awful secret that grew larger in the dark. In the presence of a supportive human circle that knew exactly what I was going through, the secret dwindled and finally dried up.

In addition to breaking the power of isolation, denial, and secrecy, meetings also provide the context for telling and hearing our stories. By recounting our history, we give it a shape and a form, an identity outside ourselves. We see that our story has a plotline, characters, a locale. We can trace the events that lead inevitably to our debting crisis and we start to identify patterns as we tell and retell our narratives. As we listen to the stories of other men and women at the meetings, we begin to identify common threads, similar behaviors. "You mean he did that too?" we think to ourselves, relieved we are not alone in kiting checks or applying for just one more charge card. Our sense of being just one more participant in the human condition, flawed and imperfect, brings relief and compassion for our own suffering and that of our fellow debtors.

In the telling and retelling, our stories begin to gain texture and vitality; we hear ourselves adding new chapters, increasingly able to identify behaviors, feelings, and beliefs that created what now seem like predictable outcomes. We start to have a relationship with our story; we are no longer unaware victims of our personal narrative. Rather, we can befriend our story and its protagonist and see what we can learn from it so that our story becomes a source of transformation, a springboard to new beliefs, attitudes, and behaviors. Then our story serves us and we can serve others.

More Than Money

Our stories also have a cyclical quality. The more we share them in our meetings, the more layers and levels we see. As my awareness grows as a result of working my program, I discover that a pattern of indebtedness I thought was about money now shows up as squandering time, selling myself short in my relationship with a friend or lover, or being anorexic in self-care. As I keep telling my narrative, with its new twists, my evolving awareness allows me to hear the narrative more deeply. Other men and women respond, speak to me after the meeting, identify with my situation. My consciousness expands and I start to see how debting behaviors hide out in nooks and crannies of my life. I discover the same pattern I had with money showing up in locales I thought had nothing to do with money. I begin to see this journey is not linear, moving nonstop from point A to point Z. Rather, the journey is a spiral, and I may tell the same story next month about a relationship that I told last month about money.

Even in my dismay at how profound this debting affliction is, how ever-present, I become fascinated, like a sleuth in a favorite mystery, by the clues pointing to the presence of debting patterns in my life: I notice I haven't stood my ground in an interaction with a colleague, so now I feel "less than." I have purchased a new dress without checking what's available in my spending plan for this month, so now I feel out of control, financially tipsy. I used to enjoy this feeling, but now the sanity from working my program sends out an alarm, as intrusive as my car's burglar alarm, letting me know I may be heading for a money drunk; it's time to check my plan. Then I can buy with sanity and sobriety.

Out of Isolation

Over time, I come to know the stories of many different people, but I perceive and am blessed by their commonality. I understand that we all suffer from negative programming and although we have added our own personal variations, our own idiosyncrasies, a shared affliction has brought unexpected gifts. I can even say, and mean it, that today I am grateful to be a recovering debtor. I can't imagine not knowing what I have found out in this program; I can't imagine not caring for all the wonderful people whose stories I have been touched by; I can't imagine living without the tools of the program that keep me sane and serene in a

money-mad and money-drunk culture; I can't imagine still
suffering in isolation and denial from the disease of compulsive indebtedness.

I have found it helpful, as do most recovering debtors I
know, to have a "home" meeting; that is, a meeting that I attend every week at the same time and place, where I come
to know the members and feel a sense of stability. Especially
at the beginning of recovery, turbulence and instability are
the norm, and establishing a regular place where I felt se-
cure and supported helped me get on the road to financial
sobriety. The first months of my recovery, I made sure I attended at least two meetings a week. I needed as much
input as I could get from people with more experience and
strength than I. I felt as if I were detoxifying the old, poiso-
nous attitudes, and I could safely dump the old financial
garbage and get the nutrients I needed from people who
had what I wanted.

By attending the same meeting regularly, I also began to
form relationships with trustworthy people who later
would serve on pressure groups for me, who would listen
and share their experience when I phoned between meetings. Some of these program buddies became close, personal
friends. I started looking forward to hearing the "shares" of
certain people whom I could count on for words of insight,
wisdom, and clarity.

Some people prefer small meetings, where everyone gets
to talk at every meeting and there is an air of informality and
intimacy. Others find comfort in a large meeting, where
there may be a greater sense of anonymity and there is only
time for some of the attendees to share at each meeting.
Early in my recovery, a wise woman said to me, "If you

don't talk, you won't get better." Over the years, I have made it a point to share at every meeting (with perhaps three exceptions) I have attended—even if my throat was dry and my heart was pounding. Something magical happens when I can say out loud to empathetic listeners what is in my heart. I have so often found that the demons haunting my soul have simply lost their power after I have called their bluff and aired my pain in community.

Meetings also let me know what I can expect down the road. They are the way I hear from others that it does get better, that a spending record will give me clarity, a spending plan will give me choices I've never seen before, and that a pressure relief group will take the pressure off of my situation with my creditors. It is in meetings that I first heard "Miracles are commonplace in this program," and before I had time to disbelieve it, saw the truth of it in the changed lives before my eyes.

I not only needed miracles, however; I also needed hard facts, reliable information that would aid my recovery. It was news to me that I could actually rent a car without a credit card, that I could negotiate with the IRS, that once a creditor cashed a check I had sent as part of a payment plan, they were tacitly agreeing to my plan. The meetings proved to be a rich source of practical information that helped me with the nitty-gritty aspects of money management and financial recovery.

Occasionally I am asked whether recovering debtors will need to attend DA meetings for the rest of their lives. As most people with any knowledge of Twelve Step programs can tell you, attendance at meetings seems to be essential to maintaining ongoing sobriety, particularly in programs like

Alcoholics Anonymous that deal with addictive substances. The majority of recovering alcoholics I know wouldn't think of missing their regular meetings, and experience tells them that ceasing to attend meetings will eventually lead to a slip, that is, to taking a drink.

Compulsive debting does have a number of similarities to alcoholism and drug addiction, but it also has some differences. In my experience, some recovering debtors find they must attend meetings on an ongoing basis in order to remain debt-free, while others can maintain financial sobriety simply by checking in at a meeting now and then. Still others seem to be able to live a solvent lifestyle without attending meetings. Most of these recovering debtors attended meetings for years, however, and have internalized the principles of the program so thoroughly that a Twelve Step attitude toward money seems to have become a permanent part of their interior landscape.

For many longtime recovering debtors, the awareness of money-related issues has been so heightened by working the DA program that they have acquired a reliable interior barometer that lets them know when they are veering off course. If they find that their serenity and stability have been negatively affected and they feel a spending fit coming on, they know where to get help. They can attend a meeting, call a program buddy, or take an appropriate action step. Whether to attend meetings forever seems to be a decision each recovering debtor must make based on individual need and the strength of his or her recovery.

We're in It Together

Attendees at any Twelve Step program meeting will inevitably hear someone say, "This is a 'we' program." The wording of each of the Twelve Steps is plural, and the Serenity Prayer reads like this: "God, grant *us* the serenity to accept the things *we* cannot change, the courage to change the things *we* can, and the wisdom to know the difference." It is through the first DA tool—meetings—that we experience the plural nature of recovery. It is here that we discover we cannot work the program alone, that recovery depends on mutual support on which each of us can draw as we need to. Sharing common concerns inside the sanctity of a confidential meeting creates a reservoir of faith, hope, and experience available on demand. And although most men and women I know in the program believe in a Higher Power or a God of their understanding, for a number of people, the group itself acts as a form of Higher Power, a tangible source of the support they need to recover from compulsive indebtedness. As thousands of recovering debtors will tell you, "The fellowship is bigger than any problem I have."

A Spiritual Gift

It was also through meetings that I first became aware of what I have come to call the "spiritual technology" of the anonymous programs. For most of my life, I have been involved in some form of spiritual belief and practice. But it occurred to me a few years ago that the Twelve Step programs have provided me with a tremendous gift I had not received elsewhere: a form of spiritual technology that addresses particular life issues in a very specific way. It feels to me as if the Steps and the tools provide the circuitry, the practical means by which I find access to a Higher Power, to a transformative energy that alters my relationship to an unhealed area of my life—in this case, money.

It's no fun being a forty-five-year-old adolescent.
—Margie J.

Money is a mystery to most compulsive debtors; a lot of us were clueless and didn't even know what questions to ask to get help. Financially speaking, we were children or, at best, adolescents. Coming into Debtors Anonymous, then, and getting sober with our money is like starting life all over again, and it brings up a lot of fear and feelings of powerlessness. But for me there was some relief in powerlessness. I had completely run out of options and so now I had to ask for help. And because my back was against the wall and I saw no choices, my willingness to do what program people suggested was high.

Anonymous programs are famous for slogans. "One day at a time" and "Easy does it," for example, are two of the more common phrases, even found on bumper stickers. For most of my life, I had disdained popular slogans, finding them trite and meaningless. But as a newcomer to DA, I listened carefully to men and women with solid recovery when they would say, "Take the action and let go of the result," or "Progress, not perfection." I discovered that solid wisdom lived inside these slogans and that I could use them to erase some of the old "stinking thinking" behind my debting behavior. By appropriating these catchy, easy-to-remember slogans in times when negative voices were kicking up a rumpus in my innards, I began to record new tapes and hold new interior conversations that stemmed from a sober attitude toward money. But without the audible, external voices of real people at my meetings, I could never have changed the negative messages in my head. They had lived there too long and had held too much power to die without a fight. I love what Jayle Greenleaf said on an audiotape entitled *Adult Children of Alcoholics and Money:* "You'd think if your parents were going to live rent-free inside your head, they'd at least fix up the place." The voices inside my head had created mayhem and now there was a major renovation taking place. Three of the slogans I was given in those early months in DA meetings proved to be powerful tools in helping me "fix up the place."

"One day at a time" saved my life in the early weeks of my recovery. Like most compulsive people in crisis, I was unable to live in the present. I spent hours obsessing about what disasters were about to obliterate me. I couldn't pay the rent; soon I would be homeless, one voice screamed. I couldn't make my car payment; soon I would have no way to get to work and then my car would be repossessed, another voice promised. I owed six thousand dollars to the IRS; soon they would come and take my furniture and my computer. You could never reason with the IRS, this voice alleged. This chorus went on and on, creating imminent disasters.

Program buddies assured me that the answer to my mounting panic was simply to live one day at a time, to calmly return to the present, to take care of today, which was the only day I *could* take care of. After all, yesterday was gone and tomorrow wasn't here yet. I would drive home from work or drift off to sleep repeating to myself, "I have what I need for today." Shifting the emphasis from the uncontrollable, out-of-reach future to the present day enabled me, bit by bit, to calm down enough to start living in the solution, rather than the problem. The solution began with not debting one day at a time and then learning to use the other tools of the program, all detailed in the next chapters.

Just Taking the Action

The second slogan that helped me to start living in the solution was "Take the action and let go of the result." It's one thing to understand a slogan conceptually and quite another to "get it," to live from it, to make it my own. Gradually, listening to other recovering debtors talk about how this slogan had helped them, I discovered the freedom its practice could bring. All I had control over in my life was the action I chose to take; I had no power over the result of my action, what other people chose to do in response to my action. It was a mystery to me how I had lived my whole life without knowing this truth, thinking that I somehow had power over outcomes. Living in accordance with this slogan began to bring me serenity and clarity. I was free to concentrate on what I needed to do and let go of what I thought other people should do. I couldn't control them anyway, and tying up my energy worrying about whether they were going to act the way I thought they should depleted me and brought frustration and resentment. This slogan served me particularly well when I began to negotiate with creditors and to make debt repayment plans.

Taking "Baby Steps"

The slogan "Progress, not perfection" gave me permission to go at my own pace in my recovery from compulsive indebtedness. I was already well aware of how imperfect I was at managing my money. I was merciless in my self-accusations and I needed to take what the program calls "baby steps." If the program had demanded adherence to a set of external standards, rather than allowing me to journey from the inside out, I would still be incurring debt today—rather than having seven years of solvency, having incurred no new debt, one day at a time, for the last seven years.

Finally, meetings gave me the opportunity to see how widespread and pervasive the disease of compulsive indebtedness is. Meetings educated me about the form debt takes, the ways it is incurred, the devastating effects it has on compulsive debtors—and their families. This chapter began with Susan's story and her mythology of money. Her belief that you better "get it while you can"—because the time will come when you can't get it anymore—fueled her compulsive spending, as she sought to get all she could while she had the buying power. Of course our compulsions, which have an energy and life of their own, don't want us to see that this belief system is false. They don't want us to know that under the guise of being good to ourselves, we are really doing ourselves in. Not until we unmask these false beliefs can we find sanity, serenity, and sobriety. Meetings are where the unmasking begins to take place. It is the place where we are enabled and empowered to look at the truth of our situation—with the support we need to stand the pain of seeing what we have created. It is the place where Reality begins to be revealed and where we learn to live in accordance with it. As author Patrick Carnes says in *A Gentle Path through the Twelve Steps,* "I commit to Reality at all costs knowing that is where I will find ultimate serenity."

What's Your Label?

Susan called herself a spendaholic. But there are many labels recovering debtors use to identify their own specific brand of money mismanagement. George introduced himself as an underearner. Although well educated and articulate, he was making slightly more than minimum wage in an independent bookstore in a small city in the Midwest. Because his hourly wage was so low, he was working sixty hours a week to meet his basic expenses, leaving his energy depleted and providing little time to explore other job options.

Natalie, a business owner and thirty-something mother of two toddlers, characterized herself as having an "emotional relationship with money." Her parents had used money to bribe her into good behavior as a child. Now she caught herself repeating the pattern—finding it easier at the end of a long day at her own ad agency to buy her kids whatever they wanted at the local fast-food restaurant, instead of insisting on nutritious meals at home. And because she was not a stay-at-home mom, she tended to compensate for lack of time with Tina and Todd by buying them expensive toys.

Michael, an Atlanta tax attorney, was in big trouble with the IRS, the bank, Visa, MasterCard, and half a dozen local businesses. The son of sharecroppers in the Carolinas, he had grown up poor and underprivileged. Through sheer determination and a few lucky breaks, he had gotten a good education, graduated from Columbia University Law School, and was now making big bucks. But he didn't want his children to grow up doing without, the way he had. When it came to his sons and daughters, money was no object. In a desperate need to compensate for his own childhood and to prove his worth, Michael had amassed a debt of $150,000 when he walked through the doors of DA. In his own unique way, Michael was a poverty addict. He had grown up poor, and now he was cash poor, as every paycheck went to pay down debt and interest, leaving little discretionary income.

Each of these recovering debtors learned to use the tools of the Debtors Anonymous program to change the self-defeating behaviors, attitudes, and beliefs that had landed them in debtor's prison. We will see how the program enabled them to move from debt to solvency as we explore their stories in more detail.

Exercises

I encourage you to complete the following exercises. They will help you to peel away the layers of your onion. Simply write down your first, instinctive response to each question, without pondering it. Questions 1 through 5 should take no more than five minutes to answer, while question 6 will probably take about ten to fifteen minutes to complete.

1. Thinking back over your childhood, how would you describe the attitude your family had toward money?

2. How would you describe your family's economic situation?

3. Was money discussed openly in your family or was there an air of secrecy about it?

4. Did you receive a regular allowance? If so, how much? Did it increase as you matured? What did you do with your allowance?

5. What was your family's attitude toward credit and charge cards?

6. In approximately two or more pages, write out your own personal narrative about the history of your relationship with money. It needn't be elaborate. Simply recall whatever comes to mind, jotting down the memories as they appear.

How Do I Get Out?
Stopping the Debt Cycle

> You cannot get out of debt by borrowing more money.
> — Jerrold Mundis, *How to Get Out of Debt,*
> *Stay Out of Debt and Live Prosperously*

Without attendance at meetings, the first tool of Debtors Anonymous, I would still be drowning in debt, incurring more obligations while trying to pay off the old ones as mounting interest and penalties devoured an ever-greater percentage of my income. Money would still be an unfathomable mystery and I would still be suffering in silence, not wanting anyone to know how clueless I was. I would be a living example of the common definition of insanity: I would be doing the same thing over and over, expecting a different financial result.

Meetings not only broke down my barriers of silence and secrecy, lifting me out of my self-imposed, shame-based isolation and bringing me back into the human circle; they also provided the context for naming the particular malaise I struggled with—compulsive indebtedness. In meetings I discovered the characteristics I shared with other money mismanagers, and I saw how pervasive this compulsion was. I observed that people of all socioeconomic groups, education levels, and professions struggled with debt, and that compulsive money mismanagement expressed itself in a variety of forms, from overspending to underearning to charging to self-debting to poverty addiction.

And it was in meetings that I heard firsthand the poignant stories of men and women whose experience and strength offered me hope when I had none. These powerful stories provided a perspective on compulsive indebtedness that I could have gained no other way, for they clearly showed, as Susan's story in chapter 3 did, the direct relationship between erroneous behaviors, attitudes, and beliefs and one's financial situation. When the veil of denial lifts—the veil under which we have shrouded our money misbehavior— and we see how we have conspired against ourselves through our compulsive indebtedness, we may feel nauseous, remorseful, overwhelmed. We may even run out and spend, charge, or borrow to distract ourselves from these uncomfortable emotions!

Creating a More Spacious Future

But we would not be offered the opportunity to see clearly, to lift the veil concealing our misdeeds from ourselves, if we were not ready to break the pattern. Sharing our story in a meeting helps us tell the truth about our past so we can create a more spacious future. Telling our story shows us where our indebtedness came from and how we got to where we are. Owning our personal history gives us the opportunity to make different choices and to use our past not to lay blame on ourselves or others but as a springboard to awareness and the creation of new beliefs, attitudes, and behaviors that enrich rather than deplete us.

Like other addictive and compulsive behaviors, compulsive indebtedness does not quietly go away by itself, nor does it remain at a constant level. The behavior itself, and the effects on one's life, escalate. What may have started as an occasional spending spree, an infrequent splurge on a charge card, or a small loan from a friend, becomes increasingly habitual and often involves increasingly larger sums of money. As we saw in Susan's story, the need to compulsively charge against the day when she might have no spending power eventually caused her to buy a personal luxury item nearly every business day! Susan wasn't in her financial driver's seat. She was not making conscious, healthy choices. Her feelings of deprivation and lack were running her life, and until she claimed her story, brought it out of hiding into the light of a supportive group, and became willing to have her attitudes changed, she was constantly victimized by her compulsive spending.

Admitting Our Money Mistakes

"Confession is good for the soul," says an old adage, and so we experience a sense of release and catharsis in the telling and the claiming of our past. We find admitting our money mistakes doesn't kill us after all, and now our story and our stock of lessons from the past join the common wisdom of the group and help others in ways we cannot know until someone approaches us after a meeting and thanks us for something we said, something we may not even remember saying!

Having discovered how we got into the mess we're in,

having told our story and identified the roots of our indebtedness, having felt the freedom that comes from finding out that what ails us has a name, a cause, and a cure, what do we do next?

The simplest truths are usually the most profound. What could be more clear or obvious than the observation "You can't get out of debt by debting"? Most of us compulsive debtors, however, stuck in the chaos and complications resulting from our insolvent lifestyles, trapped inside an ever-escalating spiral of indebtedness, are deaf to this truth. Compulsive debting runs our lives and forms the boundaries of our awareness. Until we hit bottom or in some other way are whacked between the eyes with the proverbial ax, we can't step outside the box we live in to grasp such a simple truth. We have a million good reasons why we can't stop debting because we have now lived inside a debting system and consciousness for so long, we believe we have to keep debting to pay our debts. And then we have to debt to be able to reward ourselves for living inside such a tight box and for paying our debts. But because there is no money left over after the bills, the debts, the interest, and the penalties, the only way to purchase our rewards is through incurring new debt.

Abstinence — The Second Tool

By the time I got desperate enough to go for help and landed in my first DA meeting, I was willing to do just about anything—even stop debting! But I didn't have a clue how to do that. I was familiar with the Alcoholics Anonymous progam's model of not taking a drink one day at a time, but I couldn't imagine living in accordance with the second tool of the Debtors Anonymous program—abstinence. In DA terms, abstinence simply means not incurring any new debt, one day at a time. No matter how insidious or self-destructive a compulsive behavior is, if we have lived habitually in servitude to this compulsion, we truly cannot imagine living without it.

Whether our problem is a physically addicting substance like alcohol, cocaine, or nicotine, or a behavior like compulsive gambling, compulsive debting, or compulsive eating, we feel as though we will die if we stop it. Our compulsion becomes a sort of companion, like a bad relationship that we just can't seem to leave behind. As long as we're in it, we feel, at least we're not alone.

Merriam Webster's Collegiate Dictionary defines *abstinence* as "voluntary forbearance especially from indulgence of an appetite or craving . . . ." In Debtors Anonymous, this means not incurring any new unsecured debt; that is, debt not guaranteed by collateral (such as a house or car); it would include "voluntary forbearance" from receiving money before it has been earned, goods or services before they have been paid for, borrowing money from institutions or persons, making purchases on a credit card, or writing postdated checks or checks on insufficient funds.

Although the forbearance the dictionary speaks of is indeed voluntary in DA, it cannot be accomplished alone. I and only I can decide that I want to avoid incurring new debt one day at a time, but then I must call on the resources of the group and my Higher Power or the God of my understanding in order to live an abstinent lifestyle. My negative programming and entrenched, self-defeating behaviors, attitudes, and beliefs are too powerful for me to change them without support.

Desire—The Only Admission Ticket to DA

When I walked through the door of my first Debtors Anonymous meeting seven years ago, I was in big financial trouble. Compulsive indebtedness was a way of life for me, but I met the *only* requirement for attendance at DA meetings: I had the desire to avoid incurring any new debt. I didn't believe I *could* avoid it when I entered that meeting, but I had the *desire* to avoid it. Since that February evening, I have not incurred any new debt, one day at a time, for seven years. This fact in itself is an astounding miracle to me.

If a recovering debtor had taken me aside that cold Tuesday evening and said, "You came into this meeting as a debtor, a financial drunk, but you will leave it as a recovering debtor; you never again have to incur a penny of new debt—if you make the commitment not to," I would have had trouble believing it. But I followed the suggestion I heard in the meeting: I came back for five more meetings, I listened, and I simply shared my situation.

The Four Parts of Abstinence

For me, abstinence, the second DA tool, had four parts: admitting I was a debtor, accepting the facts of my situation, making a commitment to abstinence, and taking action.

1. Admitting

I realized from the stories I heard in DA meetings that until I admitted, to myself and out loud to others, that I was a compulsive debtor, I could not move beyond indebtedness. I had to start where I was, not where I wished I were. In the words of the First Step of the Twelve Steps of DA, I admitted I was powerless over debt—that my life had become un-

manageable. Most of us would prefer to weasel out of such
an admission, but doing so would only prolong our misery.
Without a diagnosis, there can be no prognosis. Admitting
compulsive indebtedness, powerlessness, and unmanageability paves the way for the cure. But who wants to admit
being in such a condition? The "magic" of hitting bottom is
that it strips us of false pride and illusion and allows us to
claim the reality of where we are right now.

Upon hearing the First Step read aloud at a meeting, a
feminist friend who once attended DA with me vehemently
observed, "I didn't come all this way to be power*less*!" In response, a recovering debtor with several years under her
belt, said, "It's not that kind of powerlessness." That answer
helped me to understand that Step One doesn't ask us to be
dishrags with no backbone or willpower. It simply asks us
to see clearly what is right in front of us: the unmanageability of our lives in the area of finances. When I admit this
reality, I shed the illusion that has kept me stuck, kept me
trying harder and harder, to no avail. I literally become dis-
illusioned; that is, my illusions are removed. Admitting
what I am power*less* over enables me to seek help while at
the same time acknowledging and claiming what I am
power*ful* over.

2. Accepting

The second part of abstinence for me was acceptance. I had
had a false notion of the meaning of acceptance; somehow
I thought that if I *accepted* my compulsive indebtedness, I
would be capitulating to it, condoning it, saying it was
okay. Acceptance felt like defeat. Through the meetings
I attended, I came to a radical new understanding of the
word. To the program people I encountered, this term

simply referred to accepting the *facts* of a situation just the way they were. Acceptance was an acknowledgment of reality. For many compulsive debtors, who aren't particularly skilled at being realistic, accepting the facts is difficult. But nothing is changed until it is accepted—not condoned or sanctioned, but acknowledged and recognized.

An enchanting children's story entitled *There's No Such Thing as a Dragon,* by Jack Kent, describes a family whose home is visited by a little dragon that decides to take up residence there. Little Billy Bixbee, the only family member who acknowledges the dragon's existence, tries in vain to get his parents to admit that there is a dragon in the house. "There's no such thing as a dragon," they keep insisting. While Mrs. Bixbee must do contortions to vacuum around the dragon, the creature grows larger and larger, wreaking more and more havoc until the parents are finally forced to acknowledge its existence. Only then does the dragon shrink to its original size and behave itself. Whether we are talking about dragons or debts, the principle is the same: accepting the reality of our situation is the beginning of change. My own debt did indeed grow to the size of a threatening dragon before I admitted its existence and accepted the facts of my financial life. Then I discovered that acceptance is the gateway to freedom, for reality doesn't cease to exist just because I choose to ignore it.

3. Committing

Writing in his journal during an expedition over the Himalaya Mountains, W. H. Murray observed that he had learned:

> That the moment one definitely commits oneself,
> then Providence moves, too.

> All sorts of things occur to help one
> that would never otherwise have occurred.
> A whole stream of events issues from the decision,
> raising in one's favor all manner
> of unforeseen incidents and meetings
> and material assistance,
> which no man could have dreamt
> would come his way.

Making a commitment—to a marriage partner, a business venture, or a creative undertaking—always involves a risk, a journey into the unknown. It is a leap of faith that is an occasion for both fear and exhilaration. But until we take a stand, fate or the force cannot conspire with us to create the new relationship or undertaking. We must decide and commit first; then the changes begin and synchronicities start to occur. We create a place for something new to happen simply by our commitment; then we get out of the way and start witnessing the "miracles" that we could not have concocted if we tried. Through the power of exercising our choice, we set in motion a paradigm shift that then permits, as Murray says, "unforeseen incidents and meetings/and material assistance."

We live in a society that wants the material assistance first, before it makes a commitment. But W. H. Murray, the anonymous programs, and the world's great spiritual traditions all tell us that the commitment must come first and everything else will follow. Through our leap of faith, we set in motion the chain of events that provides what we need next.

The Twelve Step programs maintain that when we stop living in the problem and start living in the solution, then the problem goes away by itself. As I listened to people share in DA meetings, I sometimes said to myself, "Could these miracles really have happened?" But I knew that all of these people couldn't possibly be making up all of these stories; their sincerity was too clear, their voice too authentic, the principles underneath their stories too consistent.

Tom, for example, a Midwestern small business owner, reported that he had received an unexpected medical bill for $180, an amount not covered by his insurance company and an expense not included in that month's spending plan. A few days later, as he was considering where he might come up with the money for the medical bill without incurring debt, he found in his mailbox a check in the amount of $182, a rebate from the State of Michigan for overpayment of automobile insurance.

Such stories were commonplace and were clearly the result of the commitment recovering debtors had made to abstinence, to not incurring any new debt one day at a time. In W. H. Murray's words, these stories pointed to "a whole stream of events [that] issues from the decision."

4. Taking Action

As I have mentioned previously, Debtors Anonymous is usually considered to be the most action-oriented program of all the Twelve Step fellowships. To recover from compulsive indebtedness, a debtor has a variety of action tools at his disposal and a host of program buddies to help him implement them. Because money is a substance we cannot abstain from using (like we can drugs or alcohol), we need to learn new ways of handling it. We need to be re-educated and retrained in both management methods and attitudes. Such retraining requires that we take action steps appropriate to our stage of recovery.

After I admitted that I was a debtor, accepted the fact that I had accrued approximately fifteen thousand dollars' worth of unsecured debt (a figure that was escalating constantly because of interest and penalties on old debt and the incurring of new debt in a mad attempt to pay the old debt), and made a commitment to refrain from incurring any new debt, I was ready to take my first action step. *Not* incurring new debt is just as much an action as incurring debt, and I had to exercise this brand-new action step one day at a time. We all live only one day at a time, but people recovering from compulsive or addictive behaviors are usually more aware of that universal fact, because their recovery is granted to them only in the present. Living in the future is death to solvency and sobriety; it is only in the present moment that we experience recovery.

Drawing upon Outside Resources

I could not have survived those first days and weeks of not incurring any new debt without my two meetings a week, the support of program buddies, and check-ins with solvent, sober men and women. Patterns of a lifetime were being exchanged for brand-new ways of relating to money, and doing it alone was not an option. The "I" that had mismanaged money needed the wisdom and strength of my DA groups and my Higher Power in order to see a different model of healthy financial living. Until I could absorb and internalize these new behaviors, attitudes, and beliefs, I needed to lean on and draw from resources outside myself. Eventually these resources would be integrated within, and the new, stronger, solvent "I" could live a financially sober life. But in the meantime, I had to take the program's proverbial "baby steps."

Our Behavior—The Tip of an Iceberg

Daily committing to and taking the action step of avoiding new debt immediately shifted my behavior from that of a debtor to a recovering debtor, from living out of a standpoint of compulsive indebtedness to one of financial sobriety. It would take a lot longer, however, for my attitudes and beliefs to shift. Our behavior is the tip of the iceberg. It is what we see, but submerged below the surface, forming the bulk of the iceberg, are the attitudes and beliefs that cause our behaviors. As we saw in chapter 2, about the roots of our indebtedness, these less visible aspects of our relationship with money took years to develop. They cannot be changed overnight, but the process we have set in motion by committing to abstinence, by taking the action steps that change the things we can change, as the Serenity Prayer says, will organically change them in due course. In the meantime, we live one day at a time, changing our behavior by avoiding new debt. Just as a single tablespoon of yeast acts as powerful leaven for an entire loaf of bread, so the single action step of avoiding new debt acts as a sort of emotional or spiritual leaven for each debtor moving from compulsive indebtedness to solvency.

We cannot make ourselves adopt new attitudes toward money, nor can we impose new beliefs upon ourselves. What is in our control, however, is our decision to commit to abstinence and to take the action step of avoiding new debt. Then one day, taken by surprise, we will wake up to find out that through the steady, daily, unglamorous practice of abstinence, through a single, simple, profound change in our behavior, our attitudes and beliefs have followed the lead of our commitment. This process has a life of its own, and we can take actions, but we must always let go of the results, for they are out of our control. We create unmeetable expectations and set ourselves up for disappointment if we try to "manage" our recovery or set up a timetable for a cure. In my own experience, it was six months before I *felt* any different or before I could sense any radical interior shifts. If I had not kept putting one foot ahead of the other, keeping my commitment to abstinence, attending meetings, checking in with buddies, the feelings and beliefs would never have changed. I just had to keep taking the action and letting go of the outcome.

In an impatient, results-oriented culture, we may find it hard to keep on keeping on — without immediate fireworks results. But getting into debt took me a long time, and getting out takes awhile too. There are no easy or quick solutions, but all I needed was one solution that worked, and that's what I got.

Then, as we begin to change, as our commitment to abstinence changes our behavior, and our behavior changes our attitudes and beliefs, we find our circumstances changing — because this program, this process, is an inside job. On the way out of a meeting one afternoon, a friend and I were commenting on how smoothly our lives were going and how little chaos and unmanageability we were experiencing. It was a gorgeous, early spring day, and I commented on the beauty all around us. "Yes," she said, "it's a miraculous day. But the real miracle is that I'm sane enough to appreciate it."

About three years into my recovery from compulsive indebtedness, I found myself experiencing a particularly graphic example of Murray's "sorts of things [that] occur to help one/that would never otherwise have occurred." I now had the opportunity to tell the following story, which might help a newcomer, just as I had been helped when I was new in the program and desperately needed to hear someone else's strength, hope, and experience.

Planning Ahead

I had made an appointment for a 60,000–mile tune-up for my Toyota. In my debting days, I would have waited to get a tune-up until the car acted up or broke down. When I took the car in to my dealership, the odometer registering 60,014 miles, the service manager reminded me that Toyota recommended that a new timing belt be installed at 60,000 miles. He also noted that the dealership was having a special on timing belts—$199 instead of $300. In my spending plan for the month, I had allocated the $257 needed for this major tune-up, but I had not planned for a timing belt. I told the service manager the $199 wasn't in my spending plan, but I had had a timing belt snap on a freeway in the past, and I certainly didn't want to go through an experience like that again. I said I needed to sit down and play with some numbers and I'd let him know how to proceed in a few minutes.

Thanks to DA, I now had a contingency account, with funds set aside for emergencies, so I knew I could pay for the timing belt from that account. I gave the manager the go-ahead and had the service van take me home. At 4 P.M., when I phoned to see if the car was ready, my heart sank when I was told the service manager needed to speak with me. It turned out that when the mechanics had taken the car apart to change the timing belt, they discovered that my water pump was leaking and so they had replaced it for free. The manager said that I was only fourteen miles over the warranty and that he knew I was working with a budget, so he had given me a break! If I had had to pay for the water pump and labor, I would have owed an additional $300—beyond the $456 for the tune-up and the timing belt. If I had not been working my program, taking my action steps, and keeping my commitment to abstinence, the manager would never have known I was operating from a spending plan and would not have saved me $300. I once heard a person with a great deal of sobriety in DA say that when she had stopped living from scarcity, she found there was enough. If I had chosen to live from an attitude of scarcity and not gotten a new timing belt, I would never have been given a new water pump. Of course Mr. Murray doesn't know my tune-up story, but he would not be surprised to hear it because he knows that when we commit ourselves, then Providence moves too—in this case, acting as my service manager!

Making the switch from living out of compulsive indebtedness into abstinence also provides a new perspective on the behaviors, attitudes, and beliefs that have called the shots in our lives. Just as relocating to a new house, neighborhood, state, or country gives us a completely different viewpoint of our old house, neighborhood, and so on, a behavioral relocation, followed by attitude and belief changes, give us a new perspective on how we used to be.

A Fresh Perspective

As chapter 2 indicated, this Twelve Step process of growth in financial sobriety is not linear but cyclical. Coming into the program and telling our story during the first few months of our solvency gives us a fresh perspective on our situation. We see our history and its reverberations. But as we mature in the process and retell our story, our perception ripens and deepens. We keep seeing new facets of our experience that we just didn't see before. We didn't have the distance on our own experience, or we were still too close to old attitudes to see clearly.

As I have already mentioned, seven years ago I believed that Debtors Anonymous was about money and that if someone would just tell me how to balance my checkbook and put my financial house in order, I could be on my way and would stop having to attend these meetings. But, of course, I found out it wasn't just about the money; in fact, the bottom line was *not* about money. As I consistently used the first two tools of the DA program—meeting attendance and abstinence—my understanding of and perspective on my own story changed. It was a bit like looking through one of those colorful kaleidoscopes I loved as a child. Every time I gave the far end of the tube a turn, all the bits of colored glass made a little clicking sound and slid into a brand-new pattern.

Through the changes set in motion by my commitment to not debting one day at a time, I got to see my old behaviors, attitudes, and beliefs from a new vantage point. I had not been aware of my own mythology of money and how it had shaped my financial situation. I was now able to see that my compulsive indebtedness was directly related to a couple of very strong, very ingrained beliefs that were in charge of my money, beliefs I had been oblivious to.

The first sprang from a form of "poverty mentality" I had acquired as a sort of birthright. Loaded down as my

family had been with preachers of various assorted denominations, I had been rich in an intellectual and spiritual life
but not in material possessions. My child's mind had concluded that material things were of a lesser order than spiritual things and that acquiring possessions was linked to
greed. This distorted view prohibited me from learning to
provide adequately for myself, instead of relying on someone or something else to provide for me. Many ministers'
families have traditionally lived in a parsonage owned by
the church, had the utilities paid for by the church, and received a mileage allowance from the church. A friend who
knew of my financial difficulties once said to me, "You're
living as if the church were still providing for you, but it's
not."

I came to see that my "stinking thinking," as the program calls distorted reasoning, figured that if I couldn't get
what I needed by paying directly for it (since I could never
"own" my need or plan for it), I would have to get it devi-
ously. I proceeded to use loans and charge cards to get what
I needed, conspiring with my own neediness against the authoritarian taskmaster part of me to create a sort of financial
schizophrenia that inevitably resulted in indebtedness and
chaos.

As we saw with Susan, however, at some point, if it is
compulsive and driven by a tremendous emotional need
we're unaware of, indebtedness (like any other compulsion
or addiction) takes over. Then we're really in trouble because the indebtedness, and not we ourselves, is running our
life. Then we are no longer meeting what was originally a
real need. Now we're just feeding the hungry monster that
is our compulsion. A need can be met, but a compulsion or

an addiction can *never* be met. It has an eternal hunger that
can never be satisfied.

Somehow the fact that I was purchasing through debting came to be perceived by my distorted thinking as "I am
not purchasing at all." This was a great racket for a while; I
wasn't "supposed" to buy things, but I needed things, so
now I had created a system where I got things without buying them. I just went into debt for them. Compulsions are
not only voracious and unappeasable; they are also irrational
and they certainly don't think ahead to a day of reckoning.

For a compulsive debtor, borrowing, accepting goods
and services without paying for them at the time, and using
credit cards are all ways of putting distance between getting
the goods and paying for them. These behaviors cultivate a
mentality of getting something for nothing. A huge space
formed between my action (obtaining something) and the
obligation my action incurred (paying for it). As my abstinence began to change my mind-set and scour my brain of
my old, scummy thinking, I couldn't believe I had sub-
scribed to such a crazy dynamic. I started to think of my old
behavior as springing from what I called an "accordion attitude." I imagined one end of the accordion as my acquisition and the other end of the instrument as the payment for
my acquisition. Whenever I compulsively debted, the accordion expanded to its widest possible size, creating the
biggest distance possible between purchase and payment.
This accordion mentality came to be an accurate image of
my old relationship to purchasing.

Using Only Cash

The second old belief I discovered through my abstinent behavior was what I call the "filthy lucre" aspect of my personal history. If money is tainted, as I gathered it was from the way I saw it regarded, then who would want to touch the stuff? If the love of it is the root of all evil, as I had heard, why have anything to do with it if you can avoid it? When I used a credit card or in some other way avoided paying immediately and directly for services rendered, I didn't have to touch money at all! I never handled it in those interactions. I signed my name on a piece of paper, but no money changed hands.

One of the actions my sponsor instructed me to take early in my recovery was to go to the bank at the beginning of the week and withdraw the cash I needed for that week. I was to pay cash for everything; that way I would have to handle money. I would give the local deli owner $4.95 (instead of putting it on the tab) and he would give me a pastrami sandwich. What a novel idea! But the first time I went to the bank and took out money *for the whole week,* I practically had a heart attack. I was used to charging $4 worth of gas. Wouldn't my wallet explode if I stuffed $60 into it? It never exploded, but my heart rate took awhile to slow down, and my feelings of anxiety every Monday took even longer to dissipate.

But I probably learned the most about my old, distorted thinking when I sat down to cut up my credit cards—*all* of them—one evening. I took them all out of my wallet, spread them on the kitchen table, got out my scissors, and started cutting. I was not prepared for what happened. I suddenly felt as if I was drowning. My heart was palpitating, my mouth was dry, my palms were sweaty, and my hands were shaking. I managed to destroy all of the cards at one sitting, but the physical signals my body sent me told me how much value I had invested in a few small pieces of plastic. The sadness of my illusion swept over me, as I realized how much power I had given some plastic. In truth, all this plastic had ever done was harm me; it had never saved me, but I had acted as if it could. This moment was one of the most powerful, eye-opening moments in my entire recovery process. That moment was a microcosm of my entire life of compulsive indebtedness—thinking I needed something outside myself to save me because I believed I could never provide what I needed on my own.

Almost immediately after this experience, however, my shrunken world, boundaried as it was by plastic purchasing power, suddenly opened up. Just as I had experienced a paradigm shift—from living out of scarcity to living out of enough—when I committed to not incurring any new debt one day at a time, so now I began to think of ways to get what I needed without credit cards. As long as my plastic crutches had been available for me to lean on, I had been a financial cripple. Now I did some bartering, I sold some things I no longer needed, I took on a couple of odd jobs, and I did without some things I had thought I "needed" when I carried plastic in my wallet. Incidentally, compulsive debtors have difficulty distinguishing between needs and wants. The sense of self-reliance and ingenuity that bloomed for me after my initial anxiety departed made me wonder why I hadn't cut up my cards long ago. But of course I had not been ready, I reminded myself. Baby steps, not giant leaps, are the backbone of this program.

As we've already discussed, money is only the tip of the

iceberg when we are talking about compulsive indebtedness. Underneath what appears to be a purely practical, financial problem are the psychological and spiritual levels of this money malaise. In the next chapter we will see that, on an emotional and psychological level, abstinence means being a grown-up, something most compulsive debtors have not fully learned how to do. And at a deep spiritual level, abstinence means learning to live in accordance with Reality. Again, most compulsive debtors choose to ignore Reality, hoping it will go away. But it never does.

Exercises

The following exercises will take you approximately thirty to forty-five minutes. If you answer yes to at least three of the nine yes/no questions, a compulsion may be running your money life. You might want to make it a point to try out six DA meetings within the next six weeks.

1. How would you describe your relationship to money? Is it a mystery or do you feel clear about it?

2. Are there any aspects of your money life that you keep secret from everyone else? If so, what are they and why are they secret?

3. Are you ashamed of any of your behaviors around money? Explain.

4. Can you identify anything in your financial life that feels compulsive, or "driven," or do you feel as if you are in the driver's seat with money?

5. As a rule, do you pay cash or write a check on available funds for purchases or do you charge them?

6. Do you ever feel "money drunk" (that is, experience an adrenaline rush or change in mood) when you make a purchase?

7. Do you ever feel remorseful or depressed after purchasing goods or services?

8. Do you plan most of your purchases in advance or are you an impulse buyer?

9. What is the amount of your unsecured debt? Examples of unsecured debt include credit card balances, personal loans, back taxes, and cash revolving credit debits on checking accounts.

10. What percentage of your net monthly income goes to debt repayment?

11. How many credit cards do you have? What is the credit line for each card, and how much of that line have you used?

12. Have you ever felt that you would be better off not incurring any debt? When? What did you do about it?

13. Have you ever tried but been unable to stop incurring new debt?

14. Have you ever gone for help with indebtedness? If so, where did you go and what results did you get?

15. Do you believe you could stop incurring new debt if you chose to? Explain.

5

Didn't I Just Have $100?
Getting Real with Our Money
and Our Lives

I can find my Higher Power in my numbers.
—Anonymous recovering debtor

Compulsive debtors share many characteristics, but the one I see as the universal trait of money mismanagers is what the Debtors Anonymous program calls "terminal vagueness." Most men and women I have encountered with money troubles have no idea where their cash goes; it just vanishes. In my days of insolvency, a friend once said to me jokingly, "In your life, money is like a river—always flowing out." Although I laughed when she said it, I winced inwardly. Sometimes I could muster up some financial ineptness, but the truth did hurt. "Flowing out" was an understatement; "hemorrhaging" was a more accurate description of money's movement out of my life.

The first DA tool I experienced—attendance at meetings—gave me access to new possibilities. It let me know about a set of principles and Steps that thousands of people had already used to turn their money lives around. It told me that even I could experience a new relationship with money if I practiced these principles and drew on the wisdom of the DA program.

The second DA tool I used—abstinence—immediately, simply, and permanently brought my debt cycle to a screeching halt. With the support of my fellow recovering debtors, I incurred no new debt one day at a time.

The Spending Record—the Third Tool

The third tool—the spending record—brought an end to my terminal vagueness and money hemorrhages. As previously mentioned, Debtors Anonymous is a program noted for and characterized by action steps. Without taking the next action step at the appropriate time in our recovery, we will not be able to grow to maturity in our relationship with money and all that it represents—and we will probably also lose our financial sobriety at some point, returning to our old debting ways. Standing still is not an option in recovery; we either use the tools of the program or we lose our solvency.

Like meeting attendance and abstinence, keeping a spending record is a deceptively simple tool that is life-changing if practiced regularly. And like the all the other DA tools, the spending record not only changes our behavior with money; it also alters old, ineffective attitudes and beliefs. The *act* of record keeping is to our financial sensibility what exercise is to the body: it tones our fiscal muscles and makes us lean, strong, and disciplined where formerly we were flabby, weak, and slothful. The discipline of keeping the spending record may feel irksome at first, but over time the far-reaching effects of this tool will speak for themselves.

Every so often in a meeting a speaker will remind us that getting sober is like starting life all over again. It doesn't matter whether the sobriety refers to recovering from alcoholism, drug addiction, codependency, or compulsive indebtedness. Ceasing to drink, take drugs, live for someone else, or incur debt changes our lives radically at every level—in our behavior, our attitudes and feelings, and our belief systems.

Creating a Spending Record

Although I stopped incurring any new debt immediately after attending my first DA meeting, it took me a little longer to start keeping a spending record. About a month into the program, I began writing down what I heard people calling "my numbers." Every time I made a purchase or mailed a bill, I simply recorded the amount of the expenditure and what it was for. I kept my record in my day planner because I knew I wouldn't lose or misplace it. A typical list for a normal business day at that time in my life might have looked like this: bus fare—$1.25, coffee—60 cents, lunch—$4.00, DA meeting—$1.00, veggies for dinner—$3.49.

Some people wrote their numbers in a small spiral notebook; others on a single sheet of paper they stuck in a file folder when they got home. Still others used the computer program Quicken or created their own spreadsheets on the computer. It didn't matter *where* the record was kept as long as it *was* kept—on a daily basis. This simple recording of daily expenditures is the backbone of the spending record. Eventually the record is fine-tuned in a variety of ways, but it is better to start simply and practice simply rather than to do too much too soon.

I understood from the participants at my main meeting that a daily recording practice would eventually produce weekly, monthly, and even yearly totals for expenditures in a variety of categories, but even thinking about anything more complex than a daily record made me queasy in the beginning, so I kept daily records for quite a few weeks before I had the intestinal fortitude to add them up for weekly and/or monthly time periods. As my comfort level heightened, I felt less intimidated by adding up weekly and even monthly totals for expenditures in such categories as groceries, transportation, periodicals, eating out, and laundry.

It took me a couple of years to feel as if this record-keeping practice was second nature. But finally I was able, quite effortlessly, to keep complete, clear, detailed spending records like the one at the end of the chapter. This record lists all my expenditures for a one-month period during my third year of recovery in DA. Using the records in my daily planner, I added up weekly totals and then used the weekly totals to arrive at a monthly total for each category.

The Importance of Action

You may wonder, as I often did, why DA puts so much emphasis on action steps like the spending record—action steps that took time, that required a degree of commitment I sometimes wondered whether I really wanted to make, action steps I didn't *feel* like taking. And then when I felt like whining or quitting, I remembered: my way didn't work; it never had and it never would. And all the miracle stories I heard in meetings had come about only because these recovering debtors had surrendered to the truth that their way hadn't worked either. But the spending record and the spending plan, the debt moratorium and repayment plan, and all the other tools they had learned to use in Debtors Anonymous *had* worked and had brought them to lasting financial sobriety. Recalling that allowed me to pick up my pen and write down my numbers again. Maybe people who have healthy relationships with their money will never have to write down every penny they spend, but I was a compulsive debtor and I was lucky to have found a way out of my indebtedness.

The spending record does for debtors what we could not do for ourselves: it tells the truth about where the money goes. And the truth may be painful and at first unwelcome, but eventually it sets us free. The numbers on our record sheets don't lie; they show clearly not only what each penny is spent on, but also what our spending patterns are and, therefore, what we value. Spending records provide a picture of what we care about, what our interests are, whether we are providing adequate self-care, whether some unhealthy habit or compulsion is draining our resources, whether we are giving to others at our own *expense,* whether fast food has become our main source of nourishment.

Exposing the Raw Data

The spending record provides the raw data that shows us how our money life *is* rather than how we might imagine it is. It is the primary instrument for our moving from vagueness into clarity and from fantasy into reality. Someone in a meeting once said, "God is in our numbers." It took me a while to understand what that meant, but now I know. God is Truth and Truth calls us to account; Truth is always trying to set us free by showing us how things really are, so we can bring our lives into alignment with reality. Living in fantasy may be fun when we're five, or when we take a trip to Disney World, but eventually reality is going to win out, leaving our fantasy world in shreds. Our numbers can be a wake-up call; almost everything we need to know about our lives is reflected in them.

I once met a woman at a seminar who had made an unlikely career move. She had left the academic life, teaching English at a liberal arts college, for a career as a financial planner. When I asked what was responsible for the drastic change in professions, she said that she had always been fascinated by people's life stories and that originally she had wanted to teach, to work with students' words, to learn about their lives through that medium. But over the years, she said, she had become convinced she could learn even more about people's lives by working with their money, because the real narratives, the deepest levels of their lives, were revealed in their finances. The stories of where the money came from, where it went, how it was invested, what long-range plans existed for it, were more revelatory than the college compositions she had spent so much time on as a professor.

Despite my initial misgivings about writing down my expenditures, it wasn't long before I came to view the spending record as a gift, as a sort of barometer of my life, keeping me clear and accountable. As my weeks of records became months of records, I had even more data to give me helpful information about my spending patterns, information I became more adept at interpreting and using to make more sound, sane financial decisions. Until we keep records for some time, we have no idea how predictable we are, for the same patterns show up consistently. When we see our habits and patterns in indisputable black-and-white figures, we can ask ourselves, "Do I really want to spend my money this way or would I prefer to make some different choices?"

The difference between what we can learn about our patterns from perusing a record of one month's expenditures versus a record of several months' expenditures is immense. See the chart reflecting five consecutive months of spending records for an example of this distinction (page 100). I learned a lot about my habits and patterns from collating my records in this form. If I saw an imbalance in my spending, and therefore in my life, I could correct it by making new allocations and even new categories in future spending plans. (This tool will be discussed in chapter 7.)

For example, as I review my five-month record, I see that I had added a separate category for flowers, something I had never had before. I had always wanted fresh flowers in my office, but had never felt as if I "should" spend the money. So I either did without flowers or sneaked them into another category so I didn't have to own up to this desire in my life that my judgmental, parental self thought was frivolous. I used to think, "Flowers only die, don't they? Then you have nothing to 'show' for having purchased them."

My five-month record also disclosed that I was still not spending enough money on a professional wardrobe. My dress clothing wore out sooner than necessary and was not giving me enough variety. My fast-food totals for a couple of months pointed out that I was eating at delis and coffee shops more than I really cared to. Today, personal-care figures show a definite improvement over years of shorting myself in this area.

When I first began writing down my numbers, more

than seven years ago, I added up the daily figures at the end of each week. Because I was a novice at this type of accountability and because I had been so vague for so long, I needed to constantly monitor my expenses. But these days I usually add up my figures around the 15th of the month, and then again on the 30th or 31st. I have acquired a sixth sense and most of the time I know intuitively how I'm doing. Negative surprises, which used to be constant, are few and far between these days.

Paying Attention

If I had known, when I first began writing down my numbers seven years ago, that such a simple tool would have so many powerful benefits in my life, I would have welcomed the initial drudgery of record keeping. But until I had experienced firsthand the effects of this tool, I had no way of knowing that the spending record would create clarity where there had been terminal vagueness, order where there had been chaos, and simplicity where there had been only one complication after another. Although clarity, order, and simplicity began to permeate my relationship with money, they began to subtly affect other areas of my practical life too. It was as if my brain were being rewired somehow with new circuitry that streamlined and simplified what had overwhelmed me in the past.

One of the first, most immediate benefits of the spending record was that I began, for the first time, to pay attention to the practical details of life. The simple act of jotting down each expenditure every day had a carryover effect. I began to notice transactional details, for example, that I had been oblivious to before. One day on my lunch hour I was buying a paperback at a busy bookstore in Grand Central Station. When I actually stopped to count my change, rather than assuming the salesman had given me the appropriate amount, he remarked, "Do you know that you're the only customer I've had all day who counted her change?" I wanted to tell him why and how I arrived at being the only customer attentive to her change but decided against pouring forth a personal confession. It was enough that he had noticed my behavior. Without his knowing it, he had been indirectly touched by the reverberations of my spending record.

My sponsor had a habit of saying, "God is in the details." I have come to see that this observation is true: nothing is unimportant; everything matters. An apparently inconsequential action can have far-reaching effects and how I handle the smallest, most insignificant matter is indicative of how I handle other, greater matters. As I learned from a wonderful trainer in a seminar years ago, how I am in this moment, with this detail, is how I am. When I count my change and pay attention, I am becoming an attentive person, and an attentive person responds to life—not just to money—with a greater capacity for awareness and responseability than a nonattentive person.

Courage and Clarity

One day, a few months into keeping my spending record, I decided to buy enough subway tokens to last me two weeks. This behavior in itself was a departure from the past, when I would scrounge up enough money for only one or two tokens at a time. I gave the woman in the little booth a twenty-dollar bill, and she handed me ten tokens. "I gave you a twenty-dollar bill," I said firmly, not looking forward to an altercation at 8:30 on a Monday morning.

"No, you didn't; you gave me a ten," she said.

"I gave you a twenty," I insisted.

"You'll have to wait until I count all my money, then," she said, quite sure that I would not be willing to wait and also hold up a line of impatient New Yorkers in rush hour.

But I was. Seven minutes and an eternity later, she slapped ten more tokens down in front of me wordlessly and I knew my spending record had come through for me again. A few months earlier I would never have known I almost got shortchanged to the tune of ten dollars, and I certainly wouldn't have had the courage of my convictions—enough fortitude to do Monday morning battle with a token seller and get what was coming to me.

The clarity that the program in general and the spending record was cultivating in me showed up not only in my money. I noticed that it was becoming easier to prioritize demands on my time and to make decisions. I felt some of the old vagueness and confusion slipping away bit by bit, and I found it easier, just as I had with the token seller, to stand my ground because I was more clear about the appropriateness of my point of view.

I also felt as if I had more inner space in my life, for my head was not filled with the clutter and debris that accompanies a compulsive debtor wherever she goes. I was experiencing some relief from the constant obsession with money, bills, creditors, interest rates, finance charges.

Listening to other recovering debtors tell their stories in meetings, however, I discovered that a number of us had not always wanted the clarity and order that we were finding in DA. I heard over and over again, as my increasing awareness shed light on past behaviors, that one of the reasons for our compulsive indebtedness was the desire to avoid deeper emotional pain that lay concealed under the chaos created by our debt. Peeling away layer after layer of the onion was a difficult, slow process, one that we would never have chosen if our money situation hadn't gotten completely out of control and threatened to do us in entirely. Now, inevitably, as our money situation became less chaotic and demanding of our energy, the other underlying issues reared their heads.

Because his clarity and order were simplifying his money life, one man reported he now had to face, for the first time, his wife's deep, clinical depression. His chaotic finances had allowed him to avoid fully accepting this diagnosis and dealing with its implications. He had tried to do the impossible—buy his wife some happiness. Meanwhile, the mountain of accumulating debt had taken his attention away from her illness. Now that he was no longer able to hide her condition under the chaos of debt, his money life was improving and his emotional pain was getting more acute. He saw very clearly that he had used money as a distraction, he had asked money to buy his family happiness, and all he did was come to the verge of financial ruin while not changing the family situation one iota. His refusal to recognize his wife's depression, however, did not make her disease go away. Now, at least, he could begin to take Steps to admit and deal with the situation.

Achieving Balance

Another by-product of the spending record is the sense of balance and control that comes from seeing self-defeating spending patterns for what they are and making new choices about sane purchasing. Karen was a social worker who came from an alcoholic home where there was never enough—except at Christmas, when the family compensated for everything that was wrong during the rest of the year by charging through the stores on their way to creating an adrenaline holiday high. The rest of the year was spent cleaning up the financial debacle; the family thought the Christmas blowout was worth it.

Because Karen believed that Christmas was not Christmas without overextending herself financially, she repeated the family pattern, trying to buy one happy, pain-free day a year. She believed it was selfish not to give to her family the same Christmas they had given to her all through her childhood and adolescence. But when she hit her financial bottom, got help, and began looking at her numbers, she saw her debt pattern clearly. She decided she did not want to spend eleven months of the year cleaning up the financial wreckage of Christmas Day. It took a lot of courage and commitment on Karen's part, and a lot of support from her program buddies, to break a pattern that was so enmeshed in her family's history. Initially she faced a lot of resentment and ostracism for changing her behavior, choosing to live within her means, and celebrating a simple, debt-free Christmas. Karen's family hasn't completely come around to her way of thinking, but there are some signs of sanity beginning to infiltrate her siblings' holiday spending habits. Even if no one else changed at all, for her own sake, Karen needed to change her behavior and her belief about what makes a happy family holiday.

Income Tracking

Although the spending record is exactly that—a record of expenditures or outgo—as I grew in my recovery and became more skilled at and comfortable with keeping records, I added the component of record-keeping for income. Just as I had recorded my expenses each day in my daily planner, I now recorded income. When I had a salaried position, this process was very simple: every other Friday I recorded the same amount. When I was freelancing, my income was less predictable and regular, which made record keeping even more important.

Eventually, when I learned to create and use a spending plan, based on the spending record, I would learn to fine-tune the relationship between income and outgo, knowing that if my outgo exceeded my income, the result was debt. To avoid debt, I had two choices: increase my income or decrease my expenses, or both.

Ken, a radio show host in a small city, had asked for a pressure relief group to help with his employment situation. Although he had just signed a contract for a show that would bring him a salary of ninety thousand dollars a year, he was still holding down a draining, part-time position that left him little time for family, friends, or recreation. Because Ken had been doing his DA homework and keeping impeccable records, the pressure relief group could see very clearly that his salaried position was more than meeting his expenses and that his expenses were all reasonable and sufficient for his life situation. When they asked Ken why he was holding on to the other position, he admitted it was out of fear. His belief system, which held that you could never make enough money and should never turn down an offer, was based on personal history that was not relevant to his current life.

Time Is Money

Old ideas about what is "enough" were making Ken's life unmanageable, leaving him with insufficient time to meet his emotional needs. Most people I know who struggle with compulsive indebtedness are debting not only with money, but also with their time. If we spend all our time working, or if we are underearning—spending too many hours on the job for too small a return—we are not meeting our need for a balanced life. We can squander time as surely as we squander money, and although I do not personally keep a record of how I spend my time, I know people who have reaped many benefits from doing so. They recorded, in fifteen-minute segments, their exact activities, so they could move from terminal vagueness about their use of time to clarity, balance, and choice. After all, as the old adage says, "Time is money," and a spending record of time can provide clarity and choice about how we use time just as a spending record of money helps us clearly understand and make better purchasing decisions.

Gail, a sales associate for a direct marketing cosmetic company, reported one evening that she had noticed the same phenomenon occurring in her relationship with time as she had experienced in her relationship with money. She had discovered that, ironically, even though she complained about her overly full life and the juggling act she was constantly doing to make space for all her activities, she was really afraid of empty time and space. She enjoyed the adrenaline rush of too much activity, for it took her mind off of the emptiness of unplanned time, the lack she might feel if her time were not filled. Not until Gail had identified and noticed this underlying belief, which really ran her life, could she decide to make some different choices about the "time on her hands." Like Ken, whose fear of lack kept him working two jobs when he didn't need the second income, Gail feared the emptiness of unscheduled time, so she compulsively filled it with activity for its own sake, rather than valuing her precious time and using it with discrimination.

Occasionally in a Twelve Step meeting, someone will refer to her Higher Power or the God of her understanding as Good Orderly Direction. One of the most life-changing effects I experienced from using the tools of Debtors Anonymous, especially the spending record (and later, the spending plan), was the sense of order and focus they brought. As a newcomer, I had heard recovering debtors talk about this sense of order and control that developed as they moved from living in constant chaos into a state of manageability and balance.

Some of the members recommended balancing one's checkbook within twenty-four hours of receiving the monthly bank statement. For someone like me, who had made a habit of closing out accounts and opening new ones because my records were too chaotic to decipher, balancing a checkbook within twenty-four hours of its arrival was unthinkable at first. But keeping in mind that I only had to take one Step at a time and that the goal was progress rather than perfection, I began to work toward this objective. The sense of accomplishment and order I felt when, some months later, I *did* balance my checkbook within twenty-four hours (and balanced it to the penny!) was a pivotal point in breaking part of my mythology of money—that some people have a head

for finances and some people don't, and I most certainly
don't.

Where the Money Goes

The spending record was instrumental in helping me both to
create order and balance, for the first time, in my financial
life, and to maintain it on a steady basis. As my numbers mirrored my spending behavior, I gained awareness of my expenditures on a literal level. I also saw overall patterns that
showed me how my spending practices pictured where I put
my life's energy. For example, my initial records consistently
demonstrated my excessiveness in gift giving and my ingrained tendency toward an inadequate professional
wardrobe. It was so much easier to buy for others than for
myself!

Geraldine, a medical office manager, was jolted into
awareness by her first two months of spending records,
which showed four hundred dollars' worth of charges and
penalties resulting from her habit of writing checks on insufficient funds. She was so used to living in vagueness and
disorder that she had never really seen, in black and white,
the consequences of her behavior. Although it took months
of hard work and support from her sponsor to break this
old behavior pattern, it was the monthly spending record
that had been Geri's wake-up call. When her record showed
her that 10 percent of her take-home income was going to
bad check charges, she was faced with a hard reality she had
avoided for years. She could then make a commitment to
"bookend" her check writing by phoning her sponsor
weekly to plan ahead. She would write checks only for bills
that could not be paid in cash and she would leave her
checkbook home when she went to the mall.

Simplifying Your Life

A sense of Good Orderly Direction is not limited to the financial part of life. Men and women who had been faithfully working the program found, to their surprise, that order was effortlessly starting to characterize other areas of their lives. One man reported that he had never really noticed how much chaos there was in his life—in his office, his car, his garage. Once he began to create some order in his financial life, he found himself longing for more manageability in the rest of his world.

A woman who had been using the program tools for more than a year said she had just finished a marathon closet cleaning binge, taking eight bags of clothes to Goodwill. She discovered it was out of fear that she had been holding on to things she would never wear again. As long as she had a bulging closet, she could keep at bay her fear of having nothing. But the disorder had become intolerable to her, and the manageability that she had found from keeping her spending record, balancing her checkbook, and using cash for purchases was filtering into other areas of her life.

"I am paring down, throwing out, simplifying," said Dawn, a pack rat who found it difficult to part with a rubber band. "I have discovered that my outer disorder is a symptom of my inner disorder, and if the disorderliness is in *me,* I can do something about it."

Mary Ann, a high school history teacher, described a recent celebrative bonfire, burning stacks of old papers that were cluttering up the file drawers in her den. "Every piece of paper should have a home," she said.

As we have seen, using DA tools such as the spending record to get real with our money profoundly affects other aspects of our practical lives. Practicing clarity with our money sets in motion an ordering principle that reduces chaos and fosters simplicity. And our practical, material life is not the only area in which we can expect change to occur as a result of getting clear about money.

It's Time to Grow Up

"I know I'm a grown-up; I wear a bra and get my nails done, but I feel so childish when it comes to money. If I don't like what's happening, I just close my eyes to reality and make up my own," said Cindy in the Tuesday night meeting. She was experiencing the same predictable phenomenon that other recovering debtors described—adolescence in midlife.

No matter what our addiction or compulsion, when we finally seek help to break our habit, we find ourselves acting our age; that is, the age we were when we began using, abusing, debting. As previously mentioned, getting sober—with regard to alcohol, drugs, money, or whatever else we may have used—is like starting life over again. If we were fifteen years old when we began drinking, then psychologically we will be fifteen when we first get sober. If we have been compulsively debting since the age of eighteen, then psychologically we will be eighteen when we first become sober with our money.

We expect that what we have come to call "adolescent behavior" will include at least some elements of irresponsibility and unaccountability. We also expect that what we call "mature behavior" will be characterized by responsibility and accountability. But compulsive debtors, who often spend more than they earn, overextend themselves on credit, and write checks on insufficient funds cannot be described as mature. Emotionally and psychologically they are, like Cindy, merely adolescents in grown-up bodies.

Through the use of the tools in Debtors Anonymous, we start to use "as if" behavior. By doing this, we take the Steps that will eventually make our psychological age match our chronological age. Instead of being reactive and compulsive, we will act out of choice. Instead of closing our eyes to reality, we will respond to life on life's terms.

Practicing the principles of the DA program brings about a fundamental shift in consciousness. Without this shift, nothing changes, as we can easily see by looking at bankruptcy statistics. The majority of individuals declaring personal bankruptcy each year will do so again at some time in their lives, for without the movement to maturity that working the Steps and using the tools brings, money mismanagers remain adolescents, refusing responsibility and accountability.

Alex had grown up in a wealthy family where life was cushioned by everything money could buy. Neither he nor his sister knew what it felt like to want for anything. When he was thirty, Alex's parents died within six months of each other, and he suddenly received a sizable inheritance. Because he knew nothing about managing money, had been provided for all his life, and was an active alcoholic at the time of receiving his inheritance, Alex tore through five hundred thousand dollars within four years. Eventually waking up from the alcoholic fog he had lived in for ten years, Alex discovered he was broke and clueless.

Fortunately, when he arrived in DA, Alex had already experienced the power of working a Twelve Step program, for he had been sober in Alcoholics Anonymous for eighteen months. But psychologically he was a child, with no money management skills and an attitude of entitlement—inherited from his parents along with his money. Bit by bit, with the support of program buddies and a sponsor, Alex used the tools, starting with abstinence and the spending record, to act as if he were an adult, to cultivate the maturity he had never achieved.

Today, Alex is still not able to live in the style to which he was accustomed, but he is saner than he's ever been. He keeps accurate records, he knows where his money goes, his income slightly exceeds his expenses, and he has been able to buy a secondhand car so he doesn't have to rely exclusively on public transportation. In a rare slip, he recently bounced one hundred dollars' worth of checks. When he checked in with his sponsor, he asked her if she thought it might be a good idea to apply to his bank for a CRC (cash revolving credit account), which automatically covers bounced checks. That way, Alex thought, he wouldn't have to worry if he made a little slip now and then.

"Definitely not a good idea," said his sponsor. "You're still looking for someone to make it better. A CRC would be like having Mom or Dad come in to rescue you from reality. No, you need to be clear about how much is available in your account every time you write a check. Having a CRC would just feed your tendency to debt, giving you the cushion you had as a kid." Once his sponsor pointed out the attitude behind his desire for a CRC, Alex could readily agree that the solution to the problem was to be an accountable, mature adult, responsible for himself.

My actual monthly spending records follow. Feel free to use these as a model for your own monthly spending record. By taking the time to record where your money goes, you will learn to see where you are actually spending your money.

Monthly Spending Record

Item	Week One	Week Two	Week Three	Week Four	Total
Rent	535.00				535.00
Groceries	18.62	56.88	22.70	73.10	171.30
Car Payment	110.00		110.00		220.00
Car Insurance		30.00			30.00
Debt Repayment	120.00			25.00	145.00
Restaurants	38.33	5.43	18.52	17.88	80.16
Fast Food/Coffee					0.00
Electricity/House	22.82				22.82
Gas/House		26.89			26.89
Phone	45.68				45.68
Charity	11.00	2.00	2.00	1.00	16.00
Car Maintenance	14.89				14.89
Gas/Car	8.00	6.00	12.70	6.00	32.70
Business Supplies		8.33	4.40	5.57	18.30
Laundry	6.00	7.00			13.00
Entertainment	3.75	3.75		13.25	20.75
Personal Care		52.26	3.96	25.95	82.17
Household			36.37		36.37
Appliances		10.49			10.49
Books/Periodicals	0.50	7.50	13.22		21.22
Clothing		12.00	10.00		22.00
Gifts			19.08	33.33	52.41
Health Care		10.00		10.00	20.00
Exercise/Club				40.00	40.00
Savings	50.00		50.00		100.00
Christmas				40.00	40.00
Vacation				40.00	40.00
Garden			2.00	4.00	6.00
Education	10.00	5.00			15.00
Parking		10.00			10.00
Travel				40.00	40.00
Miscellaneous					0.00
Contingency		50.00		50.00	100.00
Massage		50.00			50.00
Division of Motor Vehicles	79.00				79.00

Monthly Spending Record for Five Months

Item	January	February	March	April	May
Rent	535.00	535.00	535.00	535.00	535.00
Allowance for Grace	8.00	8.00	8.00	8.00	8.00
Charity	19.66	7.40	8.00	3.00	9.00
Gas/Car	36.01	18.65	23.02	26.00	40.00
Restaurants	108.34	105.23	90.29	121.53	206.80
Groceries	205.53	201.81	213.32	179.72	111.68
Mail/Stamps	53.93	5.09	11.45	0.00	20.76
Personal Care	153.55	61.58	60.35	26.93	312.85
Car Payment	330.00	220.00	220.00	220.00	220.00
Car Insurance	182.05	182.04	0.00	0.00	182.09
Phone	133.68	65.85	75.67	96.03	65.45
Entertainment	14.25	36.57	38.00	13.25	34.50
Household	29.90	38.51	64.40	0.00	9.64
Books and Periodicals	58.22	13.90	39.52	17.54	37.43
Clothing	0.00	28.99	0.00	20.00	48.99
Appliances	93.86	0.00	0.00	0.00	93.86
Gifts	24.22	104.41	39.49	20.30	156.80
Gas/House	19.27	17.36	24.44	25.30	19.37
Electricity	49.86	26.21	22.03	20.41	25.40
Health/Exercise	0.00	0.00	40.00	361.00	40.00
Business Supplies	0.00	0.00	21.00	6.53	0.00
Savings	100.00	100.00	100.00	100.00	100.00
Debt Repayment	225.00	229.37	210.00	0.00	210.00
Travel	442.12	199.00	0.00	0.00	0.00
Flowers	5.00	17.66	3.13	12.32	14.48
License Plates	0.00	149.00	0.00	0.00	0.00
Laundry	10.00	0.00	23.50	6.00	0.00
Miscellaneous	14.00	1.50	1.50	4.49	0.00
Fast Food	18.83	24.77	35.81	43.37	46.24
Car Care	13.33	0.00	0.00	13.33	0.00
Music	10.58	0.00	0.00	18.99	0.00
Parking/Tolls	0.00	0.00	5.00	0.00	5.22
Medical	0.00	0.00	0.00	318.00	17.89
Garden	0.00	0.00	0.00	0.00	12.25
Income Tax	0.00	0.00	0.00	100.00	0.00

Exercises

By completing the following exercises, you will begin to
expel terminal vagueness from your life and learn to cultivate the clarity that eventually makes money elastic, creating a sense of plenty. You will not be able to complete
numbers 3 and 4 until you have done number 2.

1. On a scale of one to ten (ten being the highest), how would you
   rate yourself on clarity about where your money goes each
   month?

2. As an experiment, keep a record of your daily expenses (cash
   and checks) for one month, starting today.

3. Using a spending record similar to the one on page 99, add up
   your numbers to arrive at weekly totals, then a total for the
   month. Feel free to use different categories from those listed
   in the sample record.

4. Were your expenditures for the month more than or less than
   your income for the month? Were there any totals that surprised you? Do your figures reflect an imbalance that you
   would like to correct?

6

What Am I Worth?
Money as a Metaphor

Life's gift to us is the opportunity to realize our value.
—*Each Day a New Beginning*

I will never forget the poignant narrative I heard at a meeting one night in the early months of my recovery. A woman was recounting the story of a former friend who had been staving off financial ruin for some time. He had finally come to feel that he was so hopelessly in debt that he took his own life. Overwhelmed by his situation, he was convinced that the insurance money his family would collect upon his death would be worth more to them than his own life. He saw no other way out for himself, and he believed he was giving his family an opportunity to start over with a debt-free life.

Never again did I feel disbelief when I heard someone in a meeting say that compulsive indebtedness could eventually become a killer disease. This and other stories gave me a tremendous sense of gratitude for having found a program that could replace such despair with hope. They also gave me deeper empathy for people who had not yet discovered that there was a way out. Every time we ended a meeting with the words "Let's have a moment of silence to remember the debtor who still suffers," I experienced a feeling of compassion I had not known before I heard the story of a hopeless man's suicide.

Self-Worth

After learning to use the tools of attendance at meetings, abstinence, and keeping a spending record, I encountered a tool that helped me deal directly with an issue all recovering compulsive debtors eventually discover lurking in the shadows of their money malaise: the issue of worth.

As we've already discussed, Twelve Step meeting participants commonly suggest that newcomers try attending six meetings before deciding whether the program is right for them. Sometimes it takes six meetings for someone to gain a sense of whether she can get help in this setting. Other times, someone will know right away whether this program is for him. I can vividly recall attending my first Adult Children of Alcoholics (ACOA) meeting in a small town in upstate New York in 1988. I attended not because of alcoholism in the family but because of dysfunction caused by some rigid religious attitudes. A "laundry list"—that is, a list of common characteristics of people who came from dysfunctional families—was read as part of the opening ritual. Having never attended such a meeting before, I was completely taken aback. I felt as though someone had written this list just for me and that everyone else already knew something about me that I was only just finding out.

A profound sense of relief comes with being "found out" in this way, in hearing read aloud a list of traits that I was sure only I had suffered from. And my shock of recognition told me I was absolutely in the right place; I never had to try on six meetings because I knew right away I was in the right place, almost as if I had come home to a bunch of long-lost relatives I had never known existed.

I had a similar experience when I attended my first Al-Anon meeting at the suggestion of a friend. "Why are you suggesting Al-Anon to me?" I asked. "I'm not married to an alcoholic."

"Go and see," was all she said, and trusting that she could see something about me that I could not see myself, I went.

DA—the Ph.D. of Programs

Two years later, when I finally discovered a program for people with financial problems, I instantly recognized I belonged in the rooms of Debtors Anonymous. What I didn't bargain for was the deep angst that surfaced when I first attended the meetings, an angst I have witnessed many times since among newcomers for whom the light goes on about the depth of a disease that looks as if it's "only" about money.

As I was driving home from one of those first DA meetings, I suddenly dissolved into tears. I realized then that I had thought this program would be easy, because I had already "done" two programs. But there was a lot I didn't realize. ACOA had been about becoming aware of and healing the dysfunction unintentionally created by my family of origin. Al-Anon had been about my responses to this dysfunction, the adaptations I had created to cope with the dysfunction (adaptations that I was still using, inappropriately, in current relationships). Debtors Anonymous was different from both of the other programs; it was primarily about my feelings and beliefs about my own worth and value. Any illusions about this program being easy because of my previous Twelve Step work instantly vanished. It was clear that the fact that this program was the third one I had attended didn't mean it was easy; it meant it was hard. I had to work my way up to this fellowship that is often referred to as the "Ph.D." of all Twelve Step programs.

It would take many more months of practicing the principles and using the tools of DA before I grasped the many ways in which money symbolized self-worth. As a metaphor of worth, money—in our use of it, attitudes toward it, beliefs about it, earning, spending, and saving patterns around it—was indeed a mirror of deep, interior issues that at first glance seem unrelated to money.

Money—More Than a Tangible Object

As a tangible symbol of our energy, the investment of our time and talents in return for remuneration, money is not just a physical commodity. Our emotional and spiritual values show up in what we will do to get it and how we handle it once we've gotten it. In an uncertain world, the human desire for security and certainty gets transferred to money. Many people believe that if they just have enough money, their lives can somehow be insulated or protected against life's insecurities and unpredictabilities. We like to put our risk factor into money; we like to play the stock market or take a course in day trading so we can get rich quick and protect ourselves from uncertainty. But life itself is a risk and we have so little control over it that we delude ourselves by thinking that because money is tangible, we can find in it the control and manageability we seek. We end up believing that money is *only* a static commodity rather than a powerful, symbolic entity that requires us to relate to it appropriately.

Because I had undervalued money all my life—just as many other people overvalue it—I badly needed the sanity DA provided in helping me put money in its proper place in my life. I once heard someone in a meeting say, "My mind is a dangerous neighborhood, and I shouldn't go there alone." When compulsive debtors first arrive in DA meetings, their minds truly are dangerous neighborhoods when it comes to money. Because we are unaware of the very behaviors, attitudes, and beliefs that are doing us in—these patterns are the only ones we know—we badly need a sane perspective outside of ourselves, from someone whose mind is now a safe neighborhood.

Time to Release the Pressure

Although meeting attendance is crucial in cleaning up one's interior environment, compulsive debtors also need the concentrated focus and feedback that can only be experienced by using the tool of pressure groups and pressure meetings. A pressure group includes one man and one woman who meet with a recovering debtor to focus on a specific problem or problems the debtor needs help with. The pressure group is actually a pressure *relief* group; that is, it exists to take pressure *off* of the compulsive debtor, not to add pressure to her already stressful situation. The two pressure group members must have at least ninety days of solvency (that is, of not incurring any new debt) and must have already participated in two pressure groups of their own.

A pressure group offers support by giving us a different perspective on our financial situation and then providing specific guidance tailored to our needs. The group helps us identify clearly, on paper, where we are now so we can move beyond our immediate situation into clarity and solvency. The pressure group believes in us when we feel we cannot believe in ourselves.

The pressure relief meeting usually takes place in a neutral space where there are no interrupting stimuli. A DA meeting room not in use, a room in a church, or even a quiet corner in a coffee shop usually provides a safe, anonymous place to meet. The meeting usually lasts from one and a half to two hours, and it addresses the concerns of the recovering debtor who has requested the meeting. Typically, a newcomer to Debtors Anonymous will attend at least six DA meetings before requesting a pressure group meeting. Some people wait several months before using this recovery tool. These first weeks or months in DA give the newcomer an opportunity to listen, to absorb information about the principles and tools of the program, and to begin practicing abstinence and keeping a spending record. It also gives him the opportunity to identify potential pressure group members from among the people he hears telling their stories and sharing their experience, strength, and hope. Such men and women have usually found solutions in their own lives to problems the debtor may be currently experiencing.

Once the debtor has identified the people whose wisdom he would like to draw on to discover the solutions to his own financial problems, he speaks to each one after a meeting or perhaps calls them if their names are on the phone list. Sometimes a newcomer feels extremely intimidated by asking people for help, especially people who seem to be so much further along in the recovery process. But an essential part of each newcomer's recovery is precisely this process of asking for help and taking advantage of the hard-won wisdom of others a bit further down the road. It is also important for the newly recovering debtor to realize that "You can't keep it unless you give it away" (a slogan heard often in meetings). By asking selected individuals to serve on his pressure relief group, the newcomer is honoring their recovery and actually giving them the opportunity to keep their recovery process alive through service.

Setting Up a Meeting

Sometimes this process of setting up a pressure group is simple and sometimes it is not. It is the newcomer's job to set up the meeting. If her first choices for a pressure group say yes, then she can proceed to set up a time, place, and agenda or topic for the first meeting. If not, she would do well to not take the rejection personally, to remind herself this process is a vital part of her recovery, and then to choose another man and woman to speak with.

Once the pressure relief meeting has actually been set up, it is a good idea for the newcomer to prepare a simple agenda to help the meeting stay focused and productive. Frequently the first meeting topic is the creation of a realistic spending plan. In this case, spending records for the previous month or two would provide concrete data for the group to review. It is much easier to create a realistic spending plan that meets the newcomer's needs when it is based on actual spending records than if it is concocted in a vacuum.

Other meeting topics may include planning for requesting a debt moratorium; organizing a debt repayment plan; dealing with an emergency such as an eviction notice, an order to appear in court, or a notice from the Internal Revenue Service; planning for a career move; negotiating for a salary increase; or creating a new spending plan after debts have been paid. Examples of two different agendas brought to pressure group meetings by recovering debtors are provided on pages 111–14. One agenda includes the action steps recommended by the pressure relief group.

Whatever the subject of the meeting, the pressure group will develop an action plan by the end of the allotted meeting time. This action plan is a *suggested* plan only; no one ever *has* to follow the guidance of the group. The newcomer will usually have an intuitive sense of whether the guidance provided is sound. If it is, then the recovering debtor will probably relieve some pressure by following the action plan—a simple, step-by-step process created exclusively for his situation by people who have experienced the resolution of a similar problem. The newcomer is encouraged to ask for support, if needed, in taking each action step by phoning his pressure group members before and after taking an action.

Once a newly recovering debtor has found a sponsor, she will often ask the sponsor to be a pressure group participant, perhaps on a fairly permanent basis. Some sponsors agree to this arrangement; others prefer that their sponsoring relationship be separate from the pressure relief group relationship. It is always up to the person needing the pressure meetings to request the next meeting. Some DA members proceed on an as-needed basis; others have ongoing, regularly scheduled pressure meetings, usually on a monthly basis.

The importance of pressure group meetings cannot be overemphasized. This tool is essential to recovery from compulsive indebtedness because it applies the principles and guidelines of the DA program *directly* to one's individual situation by concentrating uninterrupted, focused time on a specific problem and finding resolution to that problem through action steps. It also lifts one person's problem out of the confines of his own limited perspective, providing space for the newly recovering debtor to start living in the solution. As the wisdom of the program points out, "When we start living in the solution, the problem goes away."

Presenting Background Material

A recovering debtor provided the following material to her pressure group to give them a clear sense of her current circumstances and a context in which to advise her on how she might create a workable spending plan, a reality-based debt repayment plan, and a plan to move toward right livelihood.

Background Material
for Pressure Relief Group Meeting

Present Situation

1. The corporation where I worked as an administrative assistant relocated two months ago, leaving me unemployed. At that position, I was just barely able to pay my bills with a little left over at the end of each month.

2. I am currently working a long-term temporary assignment at a downtown communications company. It pays twelve dollars an hour and may last for ten months. I am beginning to look for a permanent position.

3. I owe six thousand dollars in credit card debt and three thousand dollars on a student loan.

Actions Already Taken

1. Although I was turned down once, I have reapplied for unemployment benefits. I should hear soon about the results of my appeal.

2 I have sent letters to the five credit card companies I owe money to, along with a payment of twenty dollars to each one, clarifying my situation and promising to be in touch within ninety days.

3. I have filed the appropriate papers to defer my student loan.

4. I have arranged to lower my car insurance payments from two hundred fifty dollars to seventy-eight dollars a month, increasing the number of installment payments and spreading them out over a longer period of time.

Difficult Situations

1. I am delaying opening and paying bills.

2. I am not adding up my numbers to get monthly totals for my spending records.

3. I have charged about one hundred dollars' worth of small items on two of my credit cards over the last six or so weeks.

4. I do not have a spending plan.

Things I Need Right Now

1. A tune-up on my Honda

2. An appointment with the dental hygienist

3. A good pair of shoes with arch supports

Things I Need/Want within the Next Six Months

1. A suit for job interviews
2. A CD player
3. A decent bookcase

Objectives for This Pressure Group Meeting

1. Create a spending plan
2. Create a debt repayment plan
3. Help in formulating a plan to move toward right livelihood

A Different Goal

The following goal was brought to a pressure relief group by a recovering debtor who needed a new spending plan. The action steps listed are ones suggested by the pressure relief team to help the debtor create the new plan.

Goal for Pressure Relief Group Meeting, February 1995

To formulate a new spending plan—taking into consideration that of the $220 currently used for debt repayment, $150 will be available for reallocation to other categories as of April 1995. I also need to consider needs that must be met for which there is no allocation currently: medical checkups, personal-care expenses, large household expenditures, and career change expenditures.

Action Steps Recommended by Pressure Relief Group

1. Change category amounts.
    a. add contingency
    b. add medical

       c. add massage

       d. add Weight Watchers

2. Write out a visions list for household purchases.

       a. couch

       b. Quicken software

       c. other

3. Set up a fifty-dollar-per-paycheck contribution to a contingency fund.

4. Call women's health center for appointment.

5. Call Martha regarding massage.

6. Set up another pressure group meeting to review spending plan reflecting new categories.

Your Needs Come First

I vividly recall my first pressure group meeting. I chose the two people carefully. I had identified with the man, Mark, whose words of wisdom and unfailing good humor had given me rays of hope amid the bleakness of my financial situation. I also selected a businesswoman, Ellen, whose story had touched a chord in me. I had to work up the courage to ask them to serve on a pressure relief group. "Who would want to take two hours out of their busy weekend to help *me?*" I had asked myself. I was surprised and grateful when they both said yes to my request, but I had to fight off a sense of discouragement when it took several weeks to actually find a mutually agreeable time.

Looking back from my perspective of seven years of solvency, I feel compassion tinged with sadness for that newly recovering debtor who gathered the huge stack of bills she was constantly juggling and three months' worth of spending records and nervously met her pressure group at an out-door cafe one spring morning. It has been my experience, both receiving and serving on pressure groups, that our deepest money concerns—those reflecting our self-worth is-sues—inevitably show up in our pressure group meetings. How could they not? I had no idea how transparent my be-havior was to my group, but the first move I made in that meeting reflected a core belief which, at that time, I could never have articulated.

I dragged out of my briefcase a huge bundle of bills and set them on the glass tabletop. "What are those?" asked Ellen.

"My debts," I said. "I've been struggling to pay them and am late on many of them. Several have already been turned over to collection agencies."

"Put those away," she said firmly. "We're not concerned with your creditors today; we're concerned with you. You come first and when your needs have been met, then we'll address the needs of your creditors."

Taken aback, I quickly stuck the bills back into my brief-case and unearthed my spending records. I had just as-sumed my pressure group members were going to call me to account for all these debts and help me pare down my current expenditures even further. Instead, they were telling me I came first!

A Surprising Outcome

The following two hours were spent carefully reviewing my spending records, looking to see where my money cur-rently was going and whether I had listed categories that were appropriate to my needs and whether I had enough

money in each of those categories. Ellen insisted that
my paltry clothing allocation was completely inadequate for
a working woman and suggested we triple it. I was aghast.
Vacation category? I'd never thought of it. Savings? Contingency account? What was that? Entertainment? They must
be kidding.

By the time Ellen and Mark had created a spending plan
that did address my legitimate needs and did not exceed my
income, there was no money left over for debt repayment. I
was crestfallen. But they were both insistent that the only
way there ever would be enough money to repay my debts
was by taking care of my needs first. If I committed myself
to meeting my needs within the guidelines we had just out-
lined, they promised me that there would be enough money
in the not-too-distant future to begin paying debts. Our
next pressure meeting, they said, could be focused on requesting a moratorium on my debts (discussed in chapter 8).
Then, when the time was right, we could establish a debt
repayment plan.

By the time the meeting had ended, I was beset by a variety of conflicting emotions. I felt overwhelmed and grateful that two people would have given me so much of their
time and energy. I had never had anyone sit down with me
and review my finances, responding to my situation with
my best interest at heart. I also felt fearful. Was this plan really going to work? What would I do if an IRS agent
showed up at my door? I felt abashed at not being able to
pay any debts for the time being. But I also felt elated; I now
had categories I never dreamed I could have in my spending
plan—and I was authorized to spend the money. I didn't
have to sneak a hardback book or a new blouse; I was sup-

posed to spend this money from my recreation and clothing categories. (The DA tool of the spending plan will be presented in detail in chapter 7).

The behavior that I had been exhibiting, behavior that was so clear to my pressure group but so opaque to me, clearly showed my self-denigrating belief: My creditors came first; I came last. I had the cart before the horse, insisted Mark and Ellen, and I would never get out of the debt I had incurred over the last five years if I didn't put the horse first. Just as I had made the commitment to abstinence first and then found I was able to live without incurring any new debt one day at a time, so now I made the commitment to meet my needs first and then, subsequently, meet those of my creditors. Just as the commitment to abstinence had worked, so my commitment to meeting my needs worked. As I acted out an attitude of valuing myself, through using the spending plan to meet my needs, I walked myself into a new stance. I was able, with the loving support of my pressure group, who had been through all this themselves, to come to experience myself as worthy of the things and experiences I could now provide for myself, as I ceased living for my creditors and began, in an appropriate, careful way, to live for myself.

The Recovery Miracle

As the miracle of my recovery from compulsive indebtedness continued to unfold, I was eventually approached as a prospective pressure group member by newcomers who had heard me share my experience and decided they wanted what I had, just as I had heard Ellen and Mark earlier and wanted what they had.

Each pressure relief group I served on gave me the opportunity not only to use my experience to benefit others, but also to enliven my own recovery by practicing Step Twelve, which suggests that we carry the message of recovery to other debtors. Each group I served on also gave me further insight into the disease of compulsive indebtedness and showed me that underneath all the varied concerns brought to pressure meetings lay a common issue: self-worth.

Making Choices: The Red Corvette

Consistently serving on a variety of pressure groups over a period of several years gives members expertise in seeing a debtor's values manifest in his numbers. Spending records do not lie. I will never forget a dapper thirty-something businessman who had accrued forty thousand dollars' worth of debt living a fast lifestyle. After the customary six meetings, Dan brought his month's spending record to a pressure meeting. At this point he was spending more than he earned, continuing to incur new debt beyond the accrued forty thousand dollars. As the other group member and I perused the numbers, it became very clear what the financial albatross around Dan's neck was: his sports car. A full 50 percent of Dan's paycheck was supporting this red Corvette. Between car payments and car insurance, maintenance and gas, the Corvette was guzzling Dan's income, leaving him glamour-rich and cash-poor.

The goal of the meeting was to create a workable, reality-based spending plan that would meet Dan's *needs,* not necessarily all of his *wants,* while allowing him to incur no new debt. As usual, I suggested we begin by reviewing the spending record out loud, item by item. During this process it became increasingly apparent, even to Dan, that an inappropriate percentage of income was going to support his fancy car habit. But it was clear, too, that although Dan's income could exceed his expenses with one obvious, fairly simple change, he was not willing to give up his alter ego. He graciously accepted the recommendations of the pressure group, giving lip service to the suggested spending plan and action steps, but we never saw Dan at a meeting again.

Like many young professionals riding in the fast lane, Dan exhibited a common cultural attitude: "I am what I drive" or "My car is the measure of my worth." At another time in Dan's life, when he had achieved solvency and was living within his means, a Corvette might have been an appropriate vehicle for him. But facing a mountainous debt, Dan was now working to support this ego symbol—his glamorous red Corvette—rather than having his priorities ordered in such a way that he could support himself.

The Traumatic Divorce

Rebecca, a twenty-five-year-old first-grade teacher, had recently been through a traumatic divorce and found herself depressed by both the failure of her marriage and the increased financial burden most divorced people experience, at least at first. Her husband had taken the 1995 Toyota Camry when he walked out, leaving Rebecca with the 1989 Ford Taurus and a host of mechanical problems. Because Jerry, her ex-husband, had handled the accounts, Rebecca was struggling with basic money management and had bounced several checks. Her car insurance company had canceled her coverage because of nonpayment, and now she was faced with inflated rates at another insurance company.

Rebecca came into her first pressure group meeting armed with two months of spending records and a file bulging with bank statements and car insurance data. She looked like a lost teenager. It took her about three minutes to dissolve into tears. Using her spending records to get a sense of her categories and allocations, the pressure group members began to create a workable spending plan that would give Rebecca some order, stability, and control in unaccustomed financial territory.

As the group members went through the proposed plan, drawing on their experience to insert reasonable and customary amounts for each category (housing, food, car payment, clothing, personal care, and so on), Rebecca's face tightened with worry. The moment of truth in a newcomer's first pressure group meeting usually occurs when the grand total of all the category allocations becomes visible on the calculator. Will the sum of the expenditures suggested by the new spending plan exceed the recovering debtor's income? Or will the income be sufficient to accommodate the amounts in the categories? Some juggling and rearrangement of amounts can always be managed, but it certainly feels good when, on the first try, it is clear that the suggested allocations can be met by current income.

As it turned out, Rebecca's take-home income each month was $2,150.00, and her basic needs category allocations totaled $1,975.00. Rebecca could not believe it. She had so completely convinced herself that she was incapable of meeting her needs herself, and she was living in so much financial chaos and uncertainty, that she had been sure her needs would greatly outdistance her income. She felt some of her tension lessen, but more important, for the first time in her life, she realized that she could take care of herself,

that she was not an incapable financial nitwit who was forever doomed to live careening from one monetary disaster
to the next. Rebecca, who had thought of herself as worthless when it came to finances, and who felt herself to be
worthless, abandoned by her husband of three years, suddenly got a glimpse of what manageability might feel like in
her life, and her self-esteem soared.

Rebecca's pressure group wrote out a list of suggested action steps and said they would be available for telephone
check-ins. She was going to have to work hard—selling her
Taurus and looking for a good used car, being scrupulous
about staying within the category allocations, and learning to
balance her checkbook to the penny every month. Although
she did have an occasional slip now and then, overspending a
category or letting the checkbook slide, Rebecca began to use
the tools of the program to change her behavior. She soon al-
tered her old belief system—that she didn't have what it took
to manage her money and take care of herself.

I Am What I Earn

Another common belief system that reveals itself in concrete terms in pressure group meetings is the "I am what I
earn" syndrome. If the measure of our worth is the income
we produce, then how much more valuable we are if we
keep upping the income. The more we make, the more we
rely on our salary figure to define us. We feel pleased with
ourselves, even inflated, when we hear ourselves described
as being "worth" a six- or seven-figure amount.

Jon grew up in a household where the most common interaction between his parents was the sound of his mother
berating his father for not providing well enough for the
family. One day, when Jon was about five years old, he did

an errand for an elderly neighbor, who rewarded him with a quarter. Jon had never earned any money before, and he was thrilled. He thought that maybe if he ran home and gave the quarter to his mother, she wouldn't yell at his dad tonight.

There is still a note of poignancy in his voice when Jon recalls this early memory at his regular DA meeting. The not-enough-ness that characterized the emotional climate of his home, and the sense of worthlessness his father seemed to have taken on from constantly being found wanting, took root in Jon as a drivenness that blossomed years later into compulsive money-making and workaholism.

After hitting bottom from stress resulting from his workaholic behavior, Jon ended up in an inpatient treatment center where he heard about Twelve Step programs for the first time. Upon returning home after treatment, he needed support to change his lifestyle and his beliefs about money. Jon arrived at DA one night willing to do whatever it took to break his compulsive attitude toward money. Although Jon was not a compulsive debtor in the usual sense—that is, he did not accrue debt he could not pay—he did exemplify the characteristics of what the program calls a "self-debtor." He constantly shorted himself in his life—by working too hard, by spending too much, by having to work harder to pay for what he bought, by not giving himself time to foster relationships, by not developing some avocations that would rejuvenate him, by living out of control and fear, feeling that everything was up to him, that his responsibilities were almost global in nature.

Jon's first pressure group experience was very different from the usual or typical newcomer's first pressure group.

His group members advised him to *decrease* his income and commensurately decrease the amounts allocated to his spending categories. Jon needed to scale back, to simplify, to let go of his driven, goal-oriented ways. His pressure group suggested keeping a time log and then eventually developing a time spending plan to address his workaholism and to build in space for a more nourishing relational and recreational life.

Today, Jon and his wife have a three-year-old son; they have bought a sailboat and spend regular weekend time together; and they have joined a church where they have found both emotional and spiritual nourishment. Although Jon knows that the early patterns set in motion by his family of origin are a permanent part of his psychological orientation, he has a new relationship with money. Today, he has choice and balance in his life, and he has no desire to forfeit what he has found by returning to workaholism and compulsive money-making.

Exercises

The following exercises are provided to help you more deeply understand your financial situation. They will take approximately ten minutes to complete.

1. If you were asked to identify one aspect of your financial life that exerts the most pressure or stress upon you, what would you say? (For example, underearning, overspending, vagueness about outgo.)

2. Of the pressure group stories mentioned in this chapter, select the person and the situation you identify with the most. If you do not identify with any of these attitudes, create a label that names your situation. (Dan—"I am what I own"; Rebecca—"I can't take care of myself"; Jon—"I am what I earn.")

3. How do you define your worth? (For example, do you define yourself by what you own, what you earn, whom you know, what you do for a living, how hard you work, whom you are related to, what country club you belong to, what university you graduated from, where you travel, what degrees you have?)

7

What If There's Not Enough?
Money as Self-Care

Fear . . . of economic insecurity will leave us.
— The Big Book of Alcoholics Anonymous

Looking back over the tools that provide a sound structure within which a compulsive debtor can learn to live from plenty instead of from lack, we can clearly see the wisdom and common sense of the program at work. Attendance at meetings brings the debtor out of isolation and secrecy into a community that lets her know that compulsive debting is the result of negative behaviors, attitudes, and beliefs that can be identified and changed. It lets her know there is a cause, rooted in her mythology of money, and there is a cure, found in the Twelve Steps, the tools, and the action steps.

The second tool most debtors experience is abstinence. The commitment to break the debting cycle by not incurring any new debt one day at a time opens the way for the seeds of new behaviors, attitudes, and beliefs to be planted. In my experience, the third tool that is usually experienced by compulsive debtors is the spending record, which shows the record-keeper exactly where the money goes, thereby moving her from vagueness to clarity, simplicity, and order.

Typically, the fourth DA tool is the pressure group, which focuses on concrete, individual financial situations that show us how our negative beliefs about our worth are mirrored in our use of money—from putting our creditors first and ourselves last, to working eighty hours a week so we'll be twice as valuable, to earning an income to support prestigious possessions that boost our self-esteem.

As mentioned in chapter 6, a first-time pressure group often examines the spending record to provide a reality check for the compulsive debtor. Does the plan have appropriate categories and is there a sufficient amount in each category? Does the record reflect imbalances in the record-keeper's life? Do expenditures exceed income? If so, income must be increased or expenditures decreased or a combination of both. From the focused work done in the pressure group, a realistic, workable first draft of a spending plan emerges, a plan designed to meet needs, to foster balance, and to enable recovering debtors to live from a sense of worth and value rather than from a sense of worthlessness.

A Roadmap for the Future

The spending record tells us in concrete figures where our money has been going. The spending plan, however, provides a financial roadmap for the future, a set of guidelines to help us spend our money in a balanced way, a way that cultivates conscious choice, meets our needs, and enables us, perhaps for the first time, to really take care of ourselves.

Most people I know who compulsively incurred debt have spent their lives living from a sense of lack or scarcity rather than from a sense of having enough. Consequently, they have shorted themselves or gone without having needs met because they believed, consciously or unconsciously, that there was not enough. The spending plan addresses this sense of lack directly by creating the structure inside of which we *get to spend* our money. For many debtors the idea of spending money is fraught with all kinds of negative emotional baggage. In this chapter we will read the stories of several debtors whose belief in scarcity was running their lives. Their mentality of lack was changed by using a spending plan. Some debtors living out of scarcity barely spend any of their money on themselves; they pay their bills but have an anorexic relationship with money when it comes to taking care of themselves. Others believe they can only get what they need by charging. They think they must have a credit card to take care of themselves. Still others think they should take care of everyone else in the family first, often leaving themselves deprived.

Whatever the behaviors and beliefs are that lead to inadequate self-care, the spending plan changes the emphasis and shifts the paradigm from lack to plenty by specifically naming categories to meet our needs and then allocating a specific amount of money to each category. By creating a plan, with the support of a pressure group, we are given permission to take care of ourselves. Some pressure groups even suggest to the debtor that he view the resources in each category as money that *must* be spent to start changing the old not-enough belief and to move toward balance and self-care.

No More "Budget"

As a newcomer to the program seven years ago, I was particularly struck by the group's insistence that this tool be called a *spending plan* rather than a budget, because the word *budget* has the connotation of restriction, and most debtors already have a strong sense of restriction. The term *spending plan* has a completely different feeling to it, a sense of legitimizing the act of spending money in appropriate, conscious, planned ways that enable us to live balanced, solvent lives. I hadn't realized until I heard this distinction that for most of my life I had viewed spending as a negative activity. I believed one should get by with as little spending as possible, and I could see from my DA perspective where this belief had put me—in credit card hell.

A Flexible Spending Plan

The spending plan, then, empowers us by creating a structure and maintaining a system for being accountable. It does not lock us into a trap we can't escape from. This tool can be, and most often is, refined again and again as our needs change, as we become solvent and have more disposable income, as we increase our income. We delete old categories that are no longer necessary to our lifestyle and add new ones as our recovery reflects the expansion we experience on all levels—materially, emotionally, spiritually. Two years into my recovery, I added a special vacation category to my spending plan that eventually enabled me to enjoy a biking holiday I had previously only dreamed of taking. After paying off several large debts, I was able to add a computer category so I could save toward my beloved Gateway. Spending plans, like our lives, are fluid and flexible.

Marlene, a dear friend I met in graduate school, recently got married and set up a bridal gift registry with a local department store. One day she got a call from a sales associate in the gift department reporting that virtually every item she and her husband had listed had now been purchased twice. Did they want to add some new items to the registry, perhaps? Marlene said she realized at that moment that, despite the big changes she had made through the program concerning money, a residue of lack still persisted in her life and showed up when least expected. She had a limited registry because she had such limited expectations. The abundance of gifts coming her way was a complete surprise.

Another DA friend reported finally taking a planned vacation after years of merely taking the least expensive holiday possible. Instead of the customary drive to visit relatives five hours away, Sarah and her husband, Fred, flew to an out-of-state bed and breakfast that had received rave reviews in a travel magazine. The magazine itself was purchased as a result of a new category called "periodicals" in their spending plan. "As I lay down on the king-sized bed with feather pillows and a down comforter and soaked up the comfort and ambiance of this exquisite hideaway," said Sarah, "I felt an overwhelming sadness that I was just experiencing, for the first time, some of the little luxuries that make life beautiful. I was aware of the self-deprivation that was the norm in my life."

It is true that we often have no idea how we have treated ourselves until we start to experience, with the permission and legitimacy of our spending plan, some of the aesthetic, cultural, and sensuous delights we had thought we could never afford. Then the realization of how we have limited ourselves and lived from a less-than attitude may evoke sorrow and even remorse. But the good news is that there is an alternative and it is available to us; we don't have to continue to live from lack when we have the tools and support to change our behaviors and beliefs.

Once we have met with our pressure group and have

created a spending plan based on our spending records and the reality-based input of our two pressure group members, we can begin to implement the plan immediately. For me this meant continuing to keep my spending record, adding it up at the end of each week, and then seeing how I was doing, week by week, in each category, by comparing what I had actually spent to the amount of money allocated for the month in my plan.

At first I hated all this record-keeping. It felt unwieldy and confining, and I balked at the irritation of being accountable and detail-oriented. But all I had to do to get my attitude back on track was to make a phone call to a program buddy or remind myself what a mess my life had been when I was doing money my way. Then I was grateful I had a system that worked—if I would just work it.

As I kept my weekly totals and compared the cumulative total to the allocation for each category, I could gauge how much more I could spend this month in each area. If I had allocated fifty dollars for personal care and I had spent thirty-five dollars by the end of the third week of the month, then I knew I had fifteen dollars available until the end of the month. If my plan had called for me to spend twenty-five dollars on entertainment and I had spent nothing by the end of the second week, I knew I could, if I wanted to, attend the theater or see a show of Cirque du Soleil if I chose, instead of merely going to the movies. Or I might prefer to go to six movies for the matinee rate.

The Elastic Dollar

I discovered almost immediately that money was becoming elastic. As a compulsive debtor, I had experienced only tightness and constriction around money, no choice or elasticity. Now, all of a sudden, I had a lot of choices. I had the grand structure of the plan. Although the total expenditures allocated to the plan were the same as or a little less than my income, inside that basic structure I had lots of room for choice. Did I want to save my twenty-five dollar allocation for this month's entertainment and splurge next month on the supper club mystery theater, which would cost about fifty dollars? I now had a choice. Did I want to spend my arts and crafts allocation of twenty dollars on yarn for a new sweater or did I want to visit the nursery and spruce up my perennial garden?

For the first time in my life, I began to get pleasure from allocating, spending, and saving money. I could move money from one category to another; I could decide not to use my clothing allocation this month and attend a painting workshop instead. That I could have both manageability and freedom boggled my mind. I began to look forward to "doing my numbers" because the more clear I was, the more legitimate I felt about my spending and the better care I took of myself. Record-keeping began, little by little, to cease being a chore and start becoming an avenue to liberation from lack.

Over the months and years, I have ceased adding up my weekly totals and find it works for me to do one monthly total on the last day of the month. I could not have operated this way at the beginning of my recovery, but practicing the principles of the program has brought me some surprising results. I seem to have developed a sixth sense of how much I am spending and no longer need the constant feedback that I once required. I rarely encounter a surprise at the end of the month; I am almost always inside my allocation—or if I am over by ten dollars in one category, then I am under the allocation in another category.

The end of this chapter presents a spending plan kept during a period of my life when I was in transition and living very simply (page 144). Without a spending plan, I could never have felt comfortable moving from the city to the country, becoming self-employed, and paring down my lifestyle. The plan gave me clarity about what and how much I needed and let me know that I could, indeed, take care of myself with less income than I had had before in a corporate situation.

The first column lists the category of expenditure, and the second the amount of money the plan has allocated to that category. The third column lists the total amount actually spent in that category for the month. The fourth column shows a plus or minus figure; a plus figure indicates how much I have spent beyond the plan's allocation, and a minus figure specifies how much less I spent. I have then totaled the pluses and the minuses and found out exactly how much over or under the monthly plan I have gone. I also add up the total amount spent and compare it to the total amount the plan allocated for the monthly expenditure.

Although keeping all these records and performing all these calculations may seem daunting at first, I cannot imagine living without them today. These records give me freedom, balance, choice, and clarity. They bring me elasticity in my spending options and never lie to me about where the money went. They provide a sense of manageability in my financial life, and they have allowed me to experience spending as a pleasurable and absolutely legitimate way of taking care of myself. I always know how much I have and how much I have spent. Keeping records has become such second nature to me that I would no more let my end-of-month calculations slide than I would go to bed without flossing.

The Information Advantage

The spending plan and its accompanying columns have not only provided manageability and helped me develop sobriety around my money; they have also provided a wealth of information about my financial habits and patterns. The end of this chapter lists columns giving data for several months (page 145). Such comparisons let me see ongoing patterns in my money life and give me the information I need to discern any areas where I am overdoing it or underdoing it, where I am being extravagant or anorexic. I can then self correct by introducing any needed changes into the next month's plan.

For example, when I review my entertainment expenditures for four months, I see I spent next to nothing. I might want to ask myself if I am living from scarcity in this category, whether I need to plan more outings, whether I am spending time with friends at dinner parties and therefore don't currently need additional entertainment, whether I want to change the allocation to this category, and so on. Reviewing spending patterns gives me an opportunity to fine-tune my spending plan and evaluate whether I am taking care of myself and meeting my needs in a balanced way. I always have choices within this basic plan structure, so I have both freedom and boundaries.

If I notice that I consistently run ten dollars or so higher in my household allocation, I may want to increase the category allocation, or I may want to examine whether I am spending too much on Tide and SOS pads and too little on books and magazines. Again, I have information and I have a choice about how to use that information.

In addition to a spending plan and a spending record, I

keep a projection of expected monthly income and a record of actual income. I use these tools to remind myself that my outgo must not exceed my income and that if my records indicate it might, then I must increase income or decrease outgo or a combination of both. Because I have internalized these guidelines and have lived in accordance with them for a long while, I rarely have any surprises anymore—and I don't want any. I remember vividly the days when all I had was surprises, and they were almost always negative.

Having mastered the skills of keeping the spending record and the plan, I now enjoy doing my totals, seeing how I'm doing, whether I come in on target. It is okay for me to spend more than I have allocated in my plan as long as I have enough income that month to meet the expenses. Although I have learned it's not a big deal to spend ten or twenty dollars more than my plan calls for, I do need to be careful not to perpetually have a big discrepancy.

Although using the tools of the spending record and the spending plan is, for the most part, a simpler task for a single person, these vital ingredients of recovery work in marriages and significant-other relationships, as well as in families. The principles of the program are the same whether they are applied to the indebtedness of an individual, a couple, or a family. The best possible scenario, of course, is that both members of a partnership are actively involved in DA recovery. But mutual involvement does not always occur.

The next best scenario is that one partner is not actively involved in DA but is supportive of the other partner's recovery. I have served on pressure groups that included only one partner active in DA, but the other was anxious to be supportive and to reap the practical benefits of the program for the marriage or the family. In such cases, keeping a spending record and creating a spending plan is a fairly straightforward process not fraught with difficulty or disagreement. Usually the non-program partner has already seen some direct benefits as a result of the other's DA commitment and wants to use the DA tools to cultivate the solvency they have started to experience.

Difficulties may arise, however, when one partner is committed to financial recovery and the other is not, when one wants to "sober up" financially and the other wishes to remain "money drunk." Then individual solutions must be sought, usually with the help of the DA partner's pressure group. One solution that has worked for some recovering debtors in financially troubled situations is to keep their finances separate from those of their partner. Separate checking accounts and clear responsibility for specific items in the family's expenses enable the recovering partner to apply the principles of the program in her own financial life regardless of what choices her partner makes. Of course there are some situations that become so difficult that other action is required. Financial woes are often symptomatic of other deep issues plaguing a relationship. In such cases, counseling may be sought by one or both partners to see whether the issues can be resolved without ending the relationship.

A Little Something Extra

The most helpful advice my sponsor ever gave me was a guideline for dealing with unanticipated income. One-third, he said, goes to the past, one-third to the present, and one-third to the future. What he meant in literal terms was that one-third goes to debt repayment, one-third goes into my current spending plan for something I need or want right now, and one-third goes to savings. This orderly prescription for allocating extra income has saved me hours of agonizing about what to do with a small windfall. In my all-or-nothing-at-all, compulsive thinking, I would have saved it all and felt I was missing out by not having a little splurge, or I would have spent it all and felt guilty because I blew it, or I would have paid debts with it all and felt resentful because I didn't get to have any of it.

I once heard someone at a meeting observe that after a few years of attending Debtors Anonymous and living in accordance with a spending plan, he realized the reason he had never planned for allocating his monetary resources. "If you are convinced that there is not enough money to meet your needs," he said, "why would you plan?"

In addition to providing guidelines for regular monthly categories, spending plans help greatly in other situations as well. In my pre-DA days, the arrival of the car insurance invoice was always a surprise and it always caused a crisis. In my first spending plan, I put in a monthly allocation for car insurance, which I held in a contingency account and withdrew four times a year. What a relief to avoid scrambling, to have the money sitting in an account all ready to pay my premium.

Major purchases, like furniture, appliances, home repairs, or an automobile can all be planned for by inserting a category into the plan and then saving for the appropriate number of months. What a sense of satisfaction to have allocated the resources for a badly needed purchase ahead of time, instead of going into debt. Before we had a spending plan, many of us could not bring ourselves to make a cash purchase for a large item. Our fear was too great, so we debted to get what we needed instead of spending outright on an item.

In addition to making our spending aware, clear, and preplanned, the spending plan also removes that awful sense of obsession many of us debtors used to experience regularly when we considered making purchases. We might have seen something we needed, or thought we needed, and bought it on impulse or charged it. Or we might have seen it and refused to buy it, instead obsessing about the object for hours and even days. We had a push-pull relationship with spending. Virtually everything we bought—or didn't buy—was a struggle, an opportunity for self-justification or self-recrimination.

Choices, Choices, Choices

Over time, the spending plan eliminates this struggle. We no longer need to obsess about purchases because our needs are being met—in a responsible, legitimate, planned-for way. If we see an extravagant item we fall in love with, a do-or-die struggle no longer needs to occur. We can walk away, think about whether we really need or want the item, check our spending plan and see whether there is enough available or how we might borrow from another category if appropriate. We can wait twenty-four hours and decide whether we still want the item. We can call a program buddy to discuss what feelings have been stirred up and whether we are acting or reacting. We have a variety of options, which gives us a lot of space and freedom. The feeling that we *must* have this item, that it is a matter of life or

death, is a clue that something deeper is occurring emotionally. The spending plan acts as an appropriate structure and
lets us know whether and when we can legitimately make
this purchase—*if* we decide we really need or want it after
we have taken some time to consider the item—and whether
we are in the grip of a spending compulsion remaining
from a time when we believed we could never get our needs
met, that there would never be enough.

When spending plans and records had become second nature to me, my sponsor pulled a magic trick out of his bag
that I still love doing. This practice, which my sponsor devised himself, brought each month's money management
to neat, tidy closure. On the 30th or the 31st of the month,
I would look in my checkbook register to see how much
money had been available on the first of the month (usually
money left over from the previous month, typically amount-
ing to one hundred to two hundred dollars). I would then
add to that figure the total income for the month. From this
total of cash available for the month, I would subtract my
total expenditures for the month, finding out how much
money I had left over. I called this sum figure #1. Then I
would count the cash in my wallet and add this sum to my
current checkbook balance. I called this amount figure #2.
Ideally, the two figures would match.

When these two figures matched effortlessly, I felt as if
I had just won the lottery. This practice gave me an unparal-
leled sense of success and control over my finances. When
they didn't match (they were always close, however), I could
either go looking for the cause of the difference and attempt
to reconcile the figures, just as I do when I balance my checkbook, or I could be content coming close enough. This prac-

tice became a game for me, and it has honed my money management skills in a way I never thought possible. An example of a reconciliation appears at the end of the chapter (pages 145–46).

Another very useful tool, a practice my second pressure group taught me, is the mini spending plan. A sample of a plan I devised and followed is also provided at the end of this chapter (page 146); feel free to adapt it to your own needs.

Mini Spending Plans

As my pressure group and my sponsor reminded me, times of high stress or crisis can set off our old, negative spending habits. Although it produces more stress in the long run, compulsive spending often makes us feel as if we are letting off steam in the short run. We can divert ourselves from our real feelings about a situation in our lives when we indulge in spending sprees or otherwise "go unconscious." If we can identify a particular trigger that raises our blood pressure, we can plan to take some precautions and create some buffers to protect us from relapsing into old behaviors.

My sponsor strongly suggested I create a mini spending plan in preparation for the visit of a difficult relative, who would be staying in my home for five days. I recognized the turbulent feelings that were bubbling underneath my exterior and recalled that during the last visit, I had spent extravagantly, partly in a legitimate attempt to be a good hostess and partly to put a damper on emotions that could be temporarily downsized by throwing money around.

Coming up with this plan gave me the opportunity to schedule some pleasurable activities in advance, to be responsible and accountable for the cost, and to have a financially worry-free five days. Since then, I have become a fan of mini plans and use them sometimes even when I am making a day trip that has the potential to trigger old behaviors. This tool gives me a feeling of safety and allows me to stay in an attitude of choice and balance rather than unawareness. I have successfully used mini spending plans for vacations, for moving from one state to another, for weekends, for holidays.

Spending plans are powerful tools for managing our expenditures and bringing us clarity and control in our allocation of resources. But a spending plan is far more than a financial tool. It is a means for cultivating the ability to take care of ourselves, to meet our needs, to establish priorities, and to live a balanced life. Using this tool, we learn what many compulsive debtors have never learned—how to put ourselves first in a healthful way. When we put the spending plan into practice in our daily lives, we plan for self-care as well as for expenditures. The plan can even startle us into some eye-opening realizations about the behaviors, attitudes, and beliefs we have held about self-care that kept us living in lack.

One of the beliefs I uncovered through using a spending plan was the conviction that a paycheck must go to pay bills and practical expenses, as well as to buy things for others. But if I want something for myself that smacks of uselessness, something that is only for aesthetic purposes or that is purely frivolous, then I must find "other" money to use. I unconsciously had expenses separated into two categories—justifiable and unjustifiable. If I wanted something unjustifiable (like a hardback book instead of a paperback, or a bottle of perfume instead of cologne), then I had to work extra, outside my regular income, to purchase it. I was practicing a form of self-punishment rather than self-care. Learning to use a spending plan changed my old belief, allowing me to purchase, within limits, things that nourished my soul and my senses.

As Rebecca's story in chapter 6 illustrates, a belief many compulsive debtors subscribe to is that they cannot care for themselves. There is insufficient income or they don't know how to manage the income they do have and think they cannot learn. But as Rebecca learned in her pressure group meeting, although her income was limited, there was enough to support herself when she created a reasonable spending plan and made arrangements to unload her lemon of a car.

Anorexic Spending

One recovering debtor was asked by his pressure group to explain why he had made a spending plan for every pay check (there were usually two paychecks per month) rather than for every month. Only when the members of the pressure team worked with the debtor did he discover the deep-seated reason for his behavior. It was so fear-producing for him to look at all the money going out in one month that he had cut the outgo in half by putting 50 percent of the allocations into one paycheck and 50 percent into the other. Once he was aware of his fear, he could ask the group for help, make check-in telephone calls as he worked on his plan, and find that the world would not end if he allocated all his money at one time. There would still be enough.

Brad's family had owned a home furnishings company that had been highly successful and provided a lucrative income for three generations. During the years when Brad's father took over the business from his grandfather, how-ever, the company found itself in deep financial water and eventually went bankrupt. As Brad came to realize, as an impressionable teenager (he was seventeen when the com-pany went bankrupt), he had unconsciously formulated a belief system to protect himself from what felt like a dan-gerous and somewhat shameful situation. If you don't count on having money, then you won't be so disappointed, was his thinking. Accordingly, Brad had learned to scale down his expectations and, with them, his legitimate needs. His spending was so anorexic that he was not taking care of himself appropriately.

As a sales representative for a corporate office-supply company, Brad had a fluctuating income, which contributed to his "you can't count on it" belief about money. With his pressure group's input and support, he was able to create a re-alistic and adequate spending plan that he could, in fact, count on and that did meet his needs. His pressure relief team helped him distinguish between needs and wants, creating a nuts-and-bolts plan that he could rely on to meet all his basic needs. Then they added "wants" categories that could be tapped at times when Brad earned a larger income.

An Attitude of Entitlement

Veronica frequently showed up unannounced at a friend's house, laundry basket filled to overflowing. An inveterate borrower of books and CDs, she floated in and out of her friends' lives, accepting invitations to lunch or dinner, but never reciprocating. Whether she was borrowing the use of a washer and dryer or recent bestsellers from a personal li-brary, Veronica acted as though these resources were her due. She suffered (and caused others to suffer as well) from an affliction a number of compulsive debtors seem to have contracted—entitlement.

Entitlement is an attitude that produces the belief that people *owe* you. Usually it stems from a deep-seated belief that because others have and you do not have, they ought to provide. Entitlement breeds false expectations and resentment and mires a compulsive debtor in negative thinking that usually exacerbates his indebtedness—both financially and emotionally.

Although Veronica was unaware of her entitlement attitude, she came, through working with a sponsor, to some clarity about her irritating behaviors and her self-defeating attitudes. Eventually, through a lot of hard work and support from her program buddies, Veronica created a spending plan that helped her take responsibility for herself and meet her own needs, instead of sponging off of everyone else. Because she has a fifteen-dollar laundry allocation in her monthly spending plan, she doesn't show up in her friend's laundry room anymore. She also has chosen to rent an apartment of her own (she used to live with whomever she was dating in order to avoid paying rent), and she has found her way to the public library, where everyone is entitled to borrow books and CDs.

A monthly spending plan and four months of spending records follow. If you choose, you may use the following as the basis for creating your own spending plan.

Spending Plan for the Month of April

Category	Plan Amount	Actual Amount	Over/Under Plan
Rent	275.00	275.00	0.00
Phone	45.00	44.95	-.05
Electric	43.00	42.52	-.48
Debt	5.00	5.00	0.00
Car Insurance	151.00	150.50	-.50
Renters Insurance	69.00	69.00	0.00
Food	125.00	146.01	+21.01
Household	25.00	13.95	-11.05
Gas/Car	25.00	35.50	+10.50
Personal Care	15.00	11.12	-3.88
Fast Food	10.00	8.70	-1.30
Entertainment	10.00	4.25	-5.75
Gas/House	25.00	25.00	0.00
Periodicals	10.00	0.50	-9.50
Mail/Stamps	10.00	6.25	-3.75
Business	10.00	0.40	-9.60
Internet	20.00	20.00	0.00
Laundry	15.00	4.50	-10.50
Gifts	10.00	58.70	+48.70
Charity	5.00	1.00	-4.00
Clothing	20.00	64.00	+44.00
Garden	10.00	0.00	-10.00
Health	27.00	28.09	+1.09
Pets	20.00	26.24	+6.24
Education	10.00	10.00	0.00
Car Maintenance	25.00	94.80	+69.80
Restaurants	20.00	56.65	+36.65
Miscellaneous	25.00	19.00	-6.00
Yoga	20.00	20.93	+.93
IRS	82.00	82.00	0.00
Totals	1162.00	1324.56	+Total 238.92
			-Total 76.36
			Over by 162.56

Total Income for April   1556.45
Total Outgo for April   1324.56
Surplus   231.89

Four Months of Spending Records Compared to Spending Plan

Category	Plan	OCT Record	NOV Record	DEC Record	JAN Record
Rent	275.00	275.00	275.00	275.00	275.00
Phone	50.00	34.00	51.00	46.00	52.00
Electric	40.00	51.00	35.00	35.00	38.00
Debt	10.00	10.00	10.00	10.00	10.00
Food	125.00	127.00	100.00	140.00	159.00
Household	25.00	19.00	14.00	25.00	30.00
Gas/Car	25.00	23.00	32.00	24.00	37.00
Personal Care	20.00	35.00	5.00	11.00	24.00
Fast Food	10.00	2.00	15.00	6.00	18.00
Entertainment	10.00	0.00	0.00	5.00	3.00
Periodicals	5.00	0.00	0.00	5.00	10.00
Mail/Stamps	10.00	18.00	12.00	5.00	8.00
Business	30.00	33.00	8.00	2.00	1.00
Internet	20.00	20.00	20.00	20.00	20.00
Laundry	15.00	14.00	5.00	3.00	10.00
Gifts	15.00	29.00	13.00	33.00	10.00
Charity	10.00	8.00	2.00	5.00	2.00
Gas/House	25.00	25.00	25.00	25.00	25.00
Health Insurance	198.00	198.00	198.00	198.00	198.00
Clothing	10.00	0.00	5.00	0.00	20.00
Arts/Crafts	10.00	0.00	5.00	0.00	32.00
Health/Medical	15.00	0.00	10.00	0.00	17.00
Pets	20.00	20.00	18.00	27.00	17.00
Books	5.00	0.00	10.00	0.00	5.00
Miscellaneous	5.00	0.00	0.00	2.00	5.00
Car Maintenance	20.00	1.00	48.00	0.00	0.00
Restaurants	15.00	22.00	13.00	15.00	38.00
Total	1018.00	964.00	929.00	920.00	1064.00

End-of-Month Reconciliation—June 30

Available in checkbook on June 1	197.10
Total income in June	1478.88
Total	1675.98
Outgo in June	1398.14
Surplus available	277.84
Figure #1	277.84
Available in checkbook on June 30	219.65

Cash in wallet		58.19
Total		277.84
Figure #2		277.84

Figure #1 and figure #2 match; reconciliation to the penny.

Mini Spending Plan for Five Days

Day One	Gas; parking at airport	15.00
Day Two	Lunch out	20.00
	History center	12.00
Day Three	Art museum	10.00
	Dinner out	40.00
Day Four	Day trip expenses	20.00
	Dinner at inn	50.00
Day Five	Symphony	60.00
Day Six	Parking at airport	5.00
Total allocation:		232.00

Exercises

Unlike the exercises at the end of the previous chapters, questions 1, 2, and 3 of the following exercises will take several months to complete. You may want to finish reading the book and return to these exercises at a later date. Depending on what kind of records you currently keep, you may be able to answer question 4 right away. Unless you feel you need practice working a regular spending plan first, you may also want to answer question 5 right now.

1. Using two to three months of spending records, create a reality-based spending plan (not a budget) that includes enough categories with enough resources to meet your needs. Remember that your outgo cannot exceed your income. If it does, either devise a way to create additional income or to reduce expenses, or a combination of both.

2. Follow your spending plan for approximately three months, comparing your spending records to your plan and computing plus and minus totals for each category at the end of the month (see the sample on page 144).

3. Now consolidate your three months of spending records onto a spreadsheet (see the sample on page 145). What spending categories might need to be adjusted? Are you overspending in some? Underspending in others? Do you need to change your spending or your category allocations? After reviewing your data, fine-tune your plan.

4. Following the sample on pages 145–46, compare the following two figures: (1) your income for the month plus the money in your checking account at the beginning of the month (carried over from the previous month), minus your total expenditures for the month, and (2) the balance in your checking account at the end of the month plus the cash in your wallet. Do these two figures match? If there is a substantial difference, review your records to locate the source of the discrepancy.

5. Identify a situation that could benefit from the use of a mini spending plan, perhaps an upcoming vacation or weekend getaway. Create a plan and implement it. What effect did using a mini spending plan have on the situation and/or on you?

6. Can you identify a belief system you have held that may have interfered with your taking care of yourself; that is, adequately meeting your needs? Explain.

8

What Do I Owe You?
Money as a Means of Exchange

I have learned that the way my money is in any given
relationship is a mirror of that relationship.
—Muriel B., recovering debtor

Money is not merely purchasing power, although it is the
simplest way we have arrived at for buying what we need
and want. Money is not merely a measure of status or even
worth, although it carries connotations of both. Money is
also a means of exchange in transactions between and
among individuals, groups, companies, and even nations.
Money is a commodity given and received; I give the grocer
forty dollars, and he (if I am lucky) gives me two or three
bags of groceries. My employer gives me a salary and I give
her a minimum of forty hours a week and the benefit of my
education and my experience.

Out of Order

When I am in debt, when I owe money to a person or a
company, my exchange of money for goods and services is

out of order, and then my relationship with that person or entity is also out of order. If a fair and equitable exchange has not occurred, then at least one of the parties has been shorted or cheated, causing an unbalanced relationship and a variety of possible repercussions.

Because we live in a society that typically emphasizes money for its own sake, and because we worry about money *per se*, about how much we earn, how much we owe, how much we save, how much we spend, many of us have lost sight of money as a means of exchange, as something that changes hands among people—either individually or corporately. But all we really have to do to see the relational quality of money is to take a look at the resentment, confusion, and anger that builds up and blows apart relationships in which the exchange has gotten fuzzy or gone sour.

Lisa, who had asked for a pressure group meeting in order to get some help with a debt repayment plan, was trying to figure out whether she owed a former friend some money. Her friend, Amanda, had made a habit of inviting Lisa to spend the night in her apartment in the city so Lisa wouldn't have to face a long commute to the suburbs if she worked late. Little by little, what had been an occasional overnight began to be a regular routine of at least two overnights a week. Although Lisa had offered Amanda some money, the hostess had turned it down, insisting the situation did not inconvenience her at all; in fact, she enjoyed the company. Nevertheless, wanting to reciprocate in some way for her lodging, Lisa often contributed to dinner or took her friend out to a local restaurant.

One afternoon, Amanda phoned Lisa at her office. Bad weather had marooned Amanda in a nearby city, where she was making an important sales call, and she would be unable to return until the next day. She asked Lisa if she could take a cab to her apartment and feed the cats, take the dog for a walk, check the answering machine, and return any urgent phone calls, letting the callers know Amanda would return the next day.

"Gosh, Amanda," said Lisa, "I have dinner plans with an old friend out in the suburbs this evening. I wish I could help, but it's too late to make other arrangements. If you give me the names of a couple of friends here in the city, I could phone them and ask them to do it."

"Never mind," said Amanda, an edge in her voice. "You stay week after week at my apartment and now you can't even help me out for one evening when I need it?" And she slammed the phone down.

Completely bewildered by this sudden outburst, Lisa realized that Amanda, perhaps unconsciously, had been keeping score, and now she wanted to collect. All the overnights had not been free and clear after all, but Lisa had not had a clue that she had been incurring an obligation. Although she tried to follow up with Amanda and resolve the problem between them, the relationship deteriorated and eventually ended.

Lisa's pressure group assured her she did not need to add Amanda to her list of creditors to be paid, but recommended that she guard against possible future entanglements by having a clear arrangement up front if a similar situation ever arose. Because Lisa had operated in good faith and had "paid" for her room by taking her friend out, no actual debt had been accrued, although Lisa had acted with some naiveté and also perhaps with the vagueness so common to debtors.

Most of us, whether we are debtors or not, have "kept

score" with friends and relatives. We have a sort of internal scorecard or balance sheet. If my next-door neighbor asks me to pick up some milk because her car has a flat tire and the kids are starving, I probably won't mind doing it once. But if she asks me three times and yet she has never done a favor for me, or she has turned me down when I asked for a ride while *my* car was in the shop, then my scorecard says she owes me. If this pattern keeps up and I don't speak with her about it, I will probably grow a full-blown resentment, and the relationship will wilt.

Out of Balance

Money reflects a variety of stances and ways of being in a relationship. We can use money to control or be controlled; to victimize or be victimized, to dominate or be dominated. We can use money to act out problems and issues that we may not be dealing with directly in a relationship, particularly an intimate one, where the stakes of addressing an issue directly may feel too high. If our money is murky and fraught with complications in a relationship, then the relationship is undoubtedly murky too.

One young man, Charlie, whose money situation had stabilized, allowing him to work on uncovering some of the deeper issues beneath his financial patterns, described an incident that had disgusted him at the time but now he had some perspective on. One night he had received a phone call from his mother, who lived in a city two thousand miles away. She had regaled him with the usual account of family doings and then began to talk about how her dentist had been wanting to write a book on what every consumer needs to know about dental care. The dentist had just started work on his project but, having never written for publication before, he was uncertain about how to proceed.

"I was just thinking," said Charlie's mother, "that maybe you could give Dr. Krieger a call and offer him some of your editorial expertise. Maybe I could even get some free dental care out of the deal too!"

Charlie had felt his stomach lurch at the time. He knew his mother's medical insurance did not cover dental care and he was concerned for her, but he somehow didn't see this suggestion as the appropriate solution to her problem. It wasn't until much later, however, that Charlie realized how emotionally abusive his mother's attempt to use his professional expertise was. He had often been treated manipulatively, so he had felt the abuse but had been unaware of it on a conscious level. "I am beginning to really see where some of my money issues come from," he said one night in a meeting. "This is painful stuff."

Owing money and being owed money are both expressions of relationships that are out of balance. Until the inequities are addressed, more than just our financial state is in disequilibrium. As recovering debtors, if we keep working our program and using the tools available to us, we will eventually begin to deal with our creditors, pay our debts, and redress the imbalances that have become characteristic of our lives.

Standing on Firm Ground

Usually we do not attempt to repay our debts until we have achieved some stability in the program. Our main concern at first is to become solvent and to establish a firm grounding in the principles, the Steps, and the tools of Debtors

Anonymous. Until we have attended enough meetings to discover there is another way to live in relationship to money, until we have broken our debt cycle by not incurring any new debt one day at a time, until we get out of vagueness by keeping a spending record, until we receive support from a pressure group in claiming our own value, until we take care of ourselves by implementing a realistic spending plan, until we have learned to use all these tools to transform behaviors and beliefs into new ones, we are not ready to deal with creditors and repay our debts.

Requesting a Debt Moratorium

For me, as is true for most recovering debtors I know, the first stage of debt repayment was a request for a debt moratorium. This request is a communication, usually by letter, to a creditor asking for a space of time during which a "time-out" from debt repayment or dealing with debts will be observed. The letter states the amount of money due the creditor, the intention to pay the debt in full, the number of days desired for the moratorium (usually ninety days, but it can be more or less, depending on the circumstances), and specific plans for contacting the creditor at the end of the moratorium. Sometimes the communication will give a few details about the debtor's current situation and the nature of help he is getting to resolve his debt. A sample letter is provided on pages 170–71.

My pressure group helped me identify an appropriate time in my recovery to write and then mail my request to my creditors. First, I made a list of all my creditors and the amount of money I owed them. Then I composed a letter, which my group reviewed. My pressure group suggested I identify a specific person at each company or place of business whom I could contact and to whom I could send payments later on. This way I could develop a rapport and history with one individual and could avoid the runaround so common with debt situations. This suggestion proved invaluable and saved me many headaches, particularly with the Internal Revenue Service.

Not every Debtors Anonymous tool is directly linked to a specific Step from the Twelve Steps of DA, but in my experience, a request for a debt moratorium is the appropriate action step and response to Step Eight: "Made a list of persons we had harmed and became willing to make amends to them all." It took me quite a while to see my creditors as people or entities whom I had harmed; for so long I had seen them as harming me. But the more I adhered to the principles of DA, the more I began to understand that by breaking my commitment to my creditors, by not keeping my word, by copping out on my responsibility, I had in fact harmed them as well as myself. I needed to restore good faith and meet my obligations, which would benefit both creditor and debtor, but only when I was able to do so out of solvency and strength rather than debting and desperation.

The request for a debt moratorium, and the subsequent moratorium most creditors granted, provided me with a transition time in which I could acknowledge responsibility for my debts to my creditors and state my plan to pay in full, while also solidifying my relationship to the DA program and getting help from my pressure group in making a sound, realistic plan to repay my obligations. I gained some breathing space, inside a structure, something I had not had in a very long time. I had been dodging creditors, not returning phone calls, buying time, running scared. Now I had taken the first step toward a plan that would help me meet both my responsibilities to myself and also to my creditors, in that order.

I sent the same basic letter to a variety of creditors: banks, the Internal Revenue Service, credit card companies, office supply stores, small businesses, department stores, and individuals. In most cases, I did not receive an acknowledgment of my letter, but neither did I receive overt rejections or harassment. I was following one of the program maxims: "Take the action and let go of the result." I had done my part and I could not control the response I got. But I felt for the first time, in dealing with creditors, as though I had taken the initiative and was being clean and clear.

Inside the ninety-day breathing space the debt moratorium provided, I continued to work with my pressure group to develop a realistic debt repayment plan that I could implement at the end of my grace period. As keeping the spending records and living from the spending plans became second nature, I discovered that the structure and control they provided helped me take care of myself and meet my own needs. Without the solid recovery base that habitual self-care gives a compulsive debtor, she will not be able to repay debts and deal with creditors.

Debt Repayment

A wise pressure team and/or sponsor is able to help a debtor identify the appropriate time to begin debt repayment; that is, to work the Ninth Step as it applies to Debtors Anonymous. Step Nine states, "Made direct amends to such people wherever possible, except when to do so would injure them or others." In financial recovery, making amends involves assuming responsibility for the debts we have incurred by starting to pay our creditors. But we cannot pay until we are able, until it will not "injure" us. And when we do pay, we can do so only with the amount currently available in our spending plan. Otherwise, our good intentions will backfire, injuring both us and our creditors, who will find that once again, we have reneged on our promise to pay. This will further tarnish our credibility.

Once we have achieved enough financial sobriety to make a debt repayment plan, how do we actually do it? Usually, in consultation with our pressure group members, we arrive at a realistic sum of money available for debt repayment each month by checking the last several months of spending plans. Maybe we'll find we can now spend $50 a month on debt repayment. Or perhaps it will be $100. Whatever the figure, most debtors I know reported hearing a chorus of negative voices clamoring inside their head. "What good will it do to allocate $50 a month to debt repayment when I owe $10,000 to twelve different creditors? This is absurd. I will never get my debt paid off this way and my creditors will either laugh themselves silly when they get a check from me for $7.50—or they will immediately turn my account over to collection."

Our pressure team members and our sponsor have been through their own bout with negative voices and they have persisted and paid off thousands of dollars of debt by beginning small and working up. What matters is not the size of the debt but the consistent, steady practice of the principles of the program. When we simply "practice these principles in all our affairs," as Step Twelve says, we find that our debt will take care of itself. It may not be according to our time-line; but it will get repaid, in full.

A Proven Financial Formula

After we have allocated a realistic sum to debt repayment in our spending plan, then we take out our list of people we have harmed, in this case, our creditors. We need to know exactly how much we owe each one. (The end of this chapter, page 171, includes a sample list of creditors and amounts due them.) Then, usually working with our pressure group once again, we use the DA formula for debt repayment: We follow a plan that treats our creditors equally by figuring out what percentage of our total debt each creditor represents.

To help explain the formula, I have calculated debt repayment for the list of creditors on page 171. First I add up all the debts I have listed, arriving at a grand total of $10,987.33. To figure out what percentage of the total debt belongs to each creditor, I divide the amount due a particular creditor by the grand total. For example, the first amount on the list, $510, divided by $10,987.33, comes to 4.6 percent. Since $100 is available for debt repayment, I determine how much money that creditor should receive each month by taking 4.6 percent of $100, which is $4.60. When all the amounts due to individual creditors have been calculated, they should, of course, equal the total amount of due owed.

Although the derisive voices in my head may make a racket every time I write out a check for these minuscule amounts, I just keep writing, knowing that there is power in this practice and that little by little, as I consistently pay over time, the debts will get whittled away. As my recovery progresses and I reap the benefits of all the DA tools I use, I find I am able to increase the amount of money available for debt repayment without shorting myself, which could set off a compulsive debting cycle again.

Although most recovering debtors I know follow the sample formula just explained, there can be exceptions to this practice. One DA member, for example, was in such dire straits with the Internal Revenue Service that he allocated a very high percentage of his debt repayment money to back taxes. A woman whose debting behavior had created a rift with her family chose to give priority to the repayment of personal loans and followed the percentage formula only after her family's loans had been repaid.

Some people in meetings voice their discouragement over the size of their debt, feeling that they will never get out, so what's the point of implementing a plan? Another DA member will often point out that this voice is "the disease talking," and go on to say that the size of the debt is really immaterial, because the principles and tools of DA work for a debt of any size. In some cases, recovering debtors have declared bankruptcy because they felt so overwhelmed by the amount they owed. Although the DA program does not advocate bankruptcy as a way to change compulsive debting behaviors and beliefs, it never tells an individual debtor what she *should* do.

I once served on a pressure group for a young man who was as compulsive about getting out of debt as he had been about getting in. After a few months of meeting attendance, abstinence, and pressure groups, he decided this fix was too slow—so he left the program and declared bankruptcy. About six months later, he surfaced at DA again, relieved to have unloaded twenty thousand dollars in debts but having discovered that the real issues—the behaviors and beliefs that had landed him in bankruptcy court—were alive and well and were starting to run his life again. This time he made a commitment to stay in the program for the long haul. Four years later, he has had a couple of minor relapses with charge cards but has attained a level of sobriety with his money that has short-circuited his compulsive debting.

Consistency Counts

As I implemented my debt repayment plan and began whittling down the sums I owed, I noticed an interesting phenomenon: I began feeling the same compulsion to pay off my debts that I had felt about spending and charging. I longed to pay them all off *now*. I wanted to allocate larger sums to my debt repayment category and began to obsess about how I could do that. If I cut back in this spending plan category or just cut out restaurants for two or three months . . . My pressure group smiled knowingly and said they had seen this attitude surface many times. Our compulsion has given up trying to get us to charge or borrow from the bank, but now it would like us to fixate on repayment. The same frenetic energy that had gone into acquiring experiences and things was now trying to whip up a frenzy around paying them off.

My sponsor pointed out that the nature of compulsions makes it imperative that we have something outside ourselves, external to the dangerous neighborhood of our minds, that we can count on to stabilize us when we feel drunk around our money. We can be as unsober about paying off our debts as we were in incurring them, and the debt repayment plan gives us a structure that inhibits the "all or nothing at all" attitude so characteristic of someone in the grip of a compulsion. The repayment plan, like the other reliable DA tools, helps keep us steady, sane, and solvent.

Having gagged the voice screaming, "Repay faster, repay more," I kept on sending out monthly checks for what felt like shamefully small payments, but before I knew it, my balances began to reflect the results of my repayment plan. Even paying as little as $5 a month, I watched a debt of $500 shrink effortlessly to $440 by the end of the year. The sense of satisfaction I was getting from steady, long-term reduction began to replace the compulsive desire to unload all my debt immediately. I realized that it had taken me years to get into this situation and it was going to take awhile to get out. But at least I *would* get out and, with the help of the program, I would never get into debt again.

My pressure team also suggested I keep detailed records of my debt repayment. Although there were practical reasons for the records (they provided clarity and accuracy for me personally and for dealing with creditors), they acted as a tremendous morale booster. When I felt as though I had not made any progress in paying debts, I just opened my DA file and looked at the difference between the original and the current debt figures.

One set of records included a sheet for each creditor, with three columns: one for the date of a payment made, one for the amount paid, and one for the balance remaining. Another record sheet, the biggest morale booster, was a list of debts that had been fully paid. Again, three columns provided the data: one listed the name of the creditor, another the amount of the original debt, and the third, the date on which the debt had been fully satisfied.

As the amount of my debt steadily shrank and a new sense of discipline and manageability evolved from assuming responsibility for my part of the agreement I had made with creditors (by paying for the goods and services I had accepted from them), I started experiencing the fruits of "right relationship." Before I had viewed myself as a victim of preying creditors, invasive collection agents, and soaring penalties and interest rates. Taking the initiative with my creditors by requesting a debt moratorium, creating a debt repayment plan, and then consistently paying regular amounts each month allowed me to step out of my victim stance into an attitude of confidence and assertiveness. I quit running scared, jumping every time the phone rang, and piling up unopened mail. By claiming my part in the exchange I had agreed to when I incurred debt, I ceased being on the defensive and became an equal party in a financial transaction that I now had the power and the means to conclude.

An Attitude Adjustment

A forty-year-old career counselor, Lucy, had made an eight thousand dollar dent in her debt load by using the debt repayment plan when she reported that she was noticing a difference in her attitudes and feelings toward both creditors and business proprietors. She had always been too intimidated in financial transactions to question a bill or to ask for an explanation of something she didn't understand. Fearing she would be viewed as financially incompetent or, worse yet, as unable to pay, Lucy had made a practice of not making waves. On her last trip to the beauty salon, however, she found herself surprised by the amount of her bill and, without a moment's hesitation, asked for an itemization of services before writing out her check. "I couldn't believe I was asking for a breakdown," she said. "But it's my money and I need to make sure I'm getting what I pay for." Because she had begun feeling like an equal in interchanges around money, Lucy found herself effortlessly assuming assertive new behaviors.

Although the repayment plan moved me steadily out of debt, enabling me to pay off more than ten thousand dollars according to a realistic timetable that never paid my creditors at the expense of my own needs, inevitably some unpleasant and even rocky situations arose in dealing with creditors. No creditor wants to settle for ten dollars a month if he thinks he can possibly extract a larger sum from a customer. Without the support of my program in general and my sponsor and pressure team in particular, I could not have stood firm in my commitment to pay my debts in full, but according to *my plan* Pressure from both creditors and collection agents, which can prey on the fear, guilt, and shame most recovering debtors are all too familiar with, can break even the most committed people at a weak moment.

In most cases, I had obtained the name of an individual and stuck to dealing with him, both to send payments and to renegotiate payment amounts as my ability to pay grew. The regularity of the payments, which eroded the debt, did create good faith and good will with most creditors, but I came to see how important it was to have both emotional support and accurate information. If I found I was being habitually accosted by phone, I firmly told the creditor to put her communication in writing and I would respond by return mail. I had several stock phrases (which I even wrote out and kept next to the telephone) for times when I was taken unawares and didn't know what to say or how to extricate myself from an unpleasant encounter. "I'll get back to you," "Put it in writing and I will reply," or "I will check with my financial advisor and get back to you on that" all proved ways of politely closing an unwanted call.

Someone to Lean On

DA meetings are great sources of information, and it is commonplace to hear someone say, "If anyone here has experience dealing with the IRS, I'd appreciate your speaking to me after the meeting." A wealth of hard-won information was always available when I needed to know how to handle irate creditors, mounting IRS penalties, or invasive collection agents.

If I did need to speak directly to a creditor or collection agent for some reason, I wrote a script ahead of time so I couldn't be swayed from the purpose of my call, and I "bookended" my telephone call by checking in with a sponsor or pressure team member before and after speaking with the creditor. Over time the fear in the pit of my stomach subsided and I was able to speak with creditors and agents without feeling intimidated and humiliated. The survival and success stories of other recovering debtors also provided both moral support and concrete information.

Paul, a restaurant manager, had been taken to court by a major credit card company. Armed with his spending records, spending plan, paycheck receipts, and letters of communication to creditors, he faced his adversary in front of a judge. After perusing Paul's orderly records, the judge said to the credit card company's attorney, "It's clear that Mr. Donaldson is taking responsibility for his debt and is paying as much as he is currently able to. Why are you wasting my time with this matter?"

Over the course of my debt repayment, I found that the valuable information so readily available from program participants performed two functions. First, accurate information obliterates the emotional quagmire that envelops most recovering debtors who are breaking old debt payment patterns and instituting new ones. Often we had no clue how to handle the onslaught of feelings triggered by a communication from a creditor. Access to accurate information about consumer rights, the law, and what creditors and agents can and cannot do gives us some security and boundaries.

Second, accurate information was the basis for appropriate action steps on our part. As we became educated about our rights and obligations, our reality-based actions gave us the power to move confidently to pay off our debts—as we could. Discovering the fact, for example, that only the IRS can garnish wages (unless a company or individual has obtained a court order) provides some security and boundaries for a debtor being threatened by a collection agent. And this knowledge allows the debtor to use her energy to take appropriate action to reduce her debt.

There's Help Out There

The federal Fair Debt Collection Practices Act protects consumers dealing with debt collectors by spelling out exactly what collection agencies may and may not do and by providing information on what to do if a violation occurs. A brochure containing detailed information about both consumer rights and debt collection practices can be obtained from the Federal Trade Commission (FTC), Public Reference Branch, Room 130, Sixth Street and Pennsylvania Avenue NW, Washington, DC 20580. Information is also provided on the FTC's Web site at http://www.ftc.gov.

Here are some of the main prohibitions governing collection agents' practices:

- No phone calls to a consumer before 8 A.M. or after 9 P.M.
- No phone calls to a place of employment if an agent can reach the consumer at home—or if the consumer has requested the agent not to phone the place of employment
- No harrassment or threats to foreclose on home or to seize personal property, including automobiles. Three important things that a collection agent must do are

  1. identify both himself and his company
  2. state exactly what account he is attempting to collect on and how much money is owed
  3. send a letter within five days after the phone call, reiterating the content of the phone call

If these guidelines are violated, a consumer may contact the Bureau of Consumer Protection, which will investigate the complaint and ascertain whether there has been a violation of the Unfair Trade Practices Consumer Protection Law. If the law has been violated, the consumer may take the offending agency to court. A complaint may also be lodged with the Federal Trade Commission.

As recovering debtors mature in their ability to implement their repayment plan and see the fruits of their program as their debt is depleted, they also cease living from a feeling of intimidation. One woman reported that she had been awakened one Saturday morning by a collection agent. When she took a firm stand with him and asked him to put his communication in writing, he actually apologized for awakening her! She was completely taken aback—until she realized that the confidence she had gained from working her program and getting accurate information on consumer rights had communicated itself to the agent, who realized he could not intimidate her and instead showed her some respect.

Credit Cards—A National Obsession

I once attended a meeting where I was startled to hear a newcomer saddled with credit card debt share that what he did for a living was dream up ideas for a major credit card company on how to get consumers "hooked" (as he said) on charge cards! Ironically, he had fallen prey to the very traps he had helped set for others! He was finding it increasingly difficult to remain in this job, he said, because it was at such variance with the principles he was just learning in DA.

In "The Tools of Debtors Anonymous," a list of suggested actions available at DA meetings, the eleventh tool advocates maintaining "awareness of the danger of compulsive debt by taking note of bank, loan company and credit-card advertising, and by reading news accounts of its effects." The insidiousness of this particular form of incurring debt can be seen in a recent phenomenon noted by financial consultant Ruth Hayden, author of *How to Turn Your Money Life Around: The Money Book for Women* and *For Richer, Not Poorer: The Money Book for Couples.* As a guest on a broadcast of *Sound Money,* aired on National Public Radio on August 15, 1999, Hayden reported that an alarming number of college students are dropping out of school not to earn more money to pay for tuition, but to pay their whopping credit card bills! She also said statistics show that consumers who regularly use credit cards are spending one-third more than consumers who do not use credit cards.

As a recovering debtor with a less-than-perfect credit rating, I am amazed at the number and variety of credit card offers that come my way almost weekly. I have not used a credit card for seven years, and I have done all the things Visa and MasterCard would like you to believe you cannot do without a credit card. Yes, you can rent a car without a credit card; it's more time-consuming and more hassle, but it's a lot less trouble—and much less expensive—than incurring new debt. A bank debit card currently serves any need I might have for the functions of a credit card (such as ordering airline tickets by phone or getting theater tickets through the mail). All I have to do is make sure the funds are available in my checking account and then deduct the charge *at the time of the purchase.*

"You are already approved!" reads the blurb on the envelope of a Visa Classic credit card offer. "You are pre-approved!" shouts a similar MasterCard offer. And then, in recognition of my past debting behavior, another Visa offer writes me: "Congratulations! You are guaranteed approval for a Visa card with a credit limit of $300. But if you let this opportunity pass again, it may not be repeated, so please respond today!"

There's Life after Credit Cards

What these companies don't know is that I like my life just fine without credit cards. By using only the debit card, I enjoy every advantage a credit card offers without any of the disadvantages. Perhaps some day if I do a lot of international traveling, I will opt to have a credit card dedicated to travel use, but until then, life is so much simpler without credit cards that I cannot imagine why I would want one.

As we use the principles and tools of the program to right our relationships with our creditors by taking responsibility for our part of the exchange we had made, we walk ourselves into a new stance toward all forms of exchange in relationship. As some of the chaos caused by money crises fades away, there may be space for us to notice inequities in other areas of our lives. We may be giving too much or too little in exchanges involving love, attention, sex, power. Patterns we used to think characterized only our financial lives may now show up at home and at work. At first we may be disappointed or even outraged, wondering where this ends.

But we need to remember that this process is a spiral, not a straight line, and a deeper dynamic in our lives seeks our attention only when we are ready, when we have done our work in round one. We would not be presented with an opportunity to work on deeper levels if we were not ready to cultivate the principle of fair exchange in all parts of our lives.

Nora B. always introduced herself at meetings by saying she was a recovering debtor who "used men for money." Because of her position in her family of origin as "Daddy's little girl," she had become accustomed to being provided for in a luxurious manner. Like some of the recovering debtors mentioned in chapter 6, Nora did not believe she could take care of herself, especially in her accustomed style, and so she located a series of wealthy caretakers who doted on her just as her daddy had—but at a price. As she matured in her recovery, Nora was no longer willing to make the exchange necessary to perpetuate her lifestyle. Bit by bit, she moved toward self-sufficiency and self-respect by learning to meet her own needs rather than living out of emotional bankruptcy in order to acquire things. Finding that the psychological and spiritual cost of her relationships was too great, she was able to trade in the old behaviors and beliefs of a "kept woman" for new ones that did not erode her integrity and self-esteem.

Following is a sample request for a debt moratorium. Feel free to base your letter to creditors on this model.

Request for Debt Moratorium

PO Box 1000
Main Town, USA
July 21, 2000

Anybody's National Bank
PO Box 1111
Credit, CO 80161

Attention: Mr. J. L. Creditor

Dear Mr. Creditor:

I am writing to let you know that I am currently out of work and am therefore unable to make my Visa card payments. In light of my current financial situation, I am requesting a moratorium of approximately ninety days on my account. On or before October 21, I will be in touch with you about my employment status as well as a plan to resume payment of my debt. I intend to pay my bill in full and have joined a financial recovery program to get information about and support for debt repayment.

Please do not contact me by phone: I will contact you as soon as I have obtained employment and can make payments. Correspondence may be sent to the address above. I reiterate that I DO intend to pay my creditors in full as soon as possible.

Thank you for your consideration.

Sincerely,

Anonymous Debtor

Following is my first debt repayment plan discussed earlier in this chapter.

Debt Repayment Plan

Creditor	Outstanding Balance	Monthly Payment
Maureen Holcomb	510.00	4.60
Office Supply	90.00	0.80
Caterer	178.00	1.60
Book Club	75.00	0.68
Photographer	225.00	2.00
Marriage Counselor	500.00	4.50
Computer Company	200.00	1.50
Pharmacy	50.00	0.45
Sears	150.00	1.36
J. C. Penney	1500.00	13.65
Sandy Brock	650.00	5.90
J & R Auto	346.89	3.15
Visa #1	1687.21	15.30
Visa #2	2072.26	18.86
MasterCard #1	1047.50	9.53
MasterCard #2	1555.47	14.15
Jane Wylie	150.00	1.36
Total Unsecured Debt	10,987.33	
Total Monthly Debt Allocation		99.39

Exercises

These exercises will take some time to complete. It is suggested that you complete reading the book before responding to questions 1–4. Respond to question 5 (that is, completing a debt retirement sheet) as soon you have paid off an outstanding debt for the first time. Question 6 can be answered at any time.

1. Make a list of all your creditors, listing the creditor's name in one column and the amount of your debt in another column. (The list should include creditors for unsecured debts only, not for a house, car, and so on.) Total your debts, entering the amount of your entire indebtedness at the bottom of the list.

2. If you are having difficulty meeting your financial obligations or have to cut back on your legitimate needs in order to meet your monthly balances due, identify an amount for total debt repayment that would allow you to meet all your needs every month.

3. Using the amount you have identified as available for debt repayment, create a debt repayment plan modeled on the example in the chapter (page 171). You will have one column for the name of the creditor, a second column for the total amount of your debt to that creditor, and a third column for the amount you will pay the creditor on a monthly basis until the debt has been paid in full. To arrive at the amount in the third column, follow the formula provided on page 158.

4. Create a file of records, with one sheet for each creditor, listing the date of each monthly payment, the amount paid, and the balance due.

5. As you begin to retire debts, create a debt retirement sheet, listing the name of the creditor whom you have paid in full, the total amount of debt paid, and the date the debt was retired.

6. Can you identify any relationships in which the exchange between you and another (for example, employer, friend, family member) is out of balance, creating some form of debt —emotional, psychological, spiritual, or other? Explain the debting dynamic you see at work. How could you start to create an even exchange?

9

Where Do I Go from Here?
Living from a Larger Self

"Our deepest fear is not that we are inadequate. Our deepest
fear is that we are powerful beyond measure." . . . We ask
ourselves, Who am I to be brilliant, gorgeous, talented, and
fabulous? Actually, who are you not to be? You are a child of
God. Your playing small doesn't serve the world. There's nothing enlightened about shrinking so that other people won't feel
insecure around you. . . . We were born to make manifest the
glory of God that is within us. It's not just in some of us; it's in
everyone. And as we let our own light shine, we unconsciously
give other people permission to do the same. As we're liberated
from our own fear, our presence automatically liberates others.

—Marianne Williamson, *A Return to Love: Reflections on the
Principles of* A Course in Miracles

If the spending record is the Debtors Anonymous tool that
moves compulsive debtors out of vagueness and into clarity,
helping them to live in reality instead of fantasy; if the
spending plan is the tool that enables recovering debtors to
meet their needs by spending in a balanced way inside a realistic structure; if the debt repayment plan is the tool that

helps money mismanagers learn to meet their obligations and to live according to the principle of fair exchange; then the ideal spending plan is the tool that helps debtors start to live from a larger, more spacious sense of self.

Living in the Solution

When compulsive indebtedness tyrannizes our lives, boxing us in, trapping us, reducing our options, shrinking our choices, we live from a small self, a self that feels constantly diminished and reduced. But when we start to practice the Twelve Steps and to apply the principles and tools of DA to our indebtedness, when we quit living in the problem and start living in the solution, then we gradually start to cultivate a larger self, a self that has emerged from the entrapment of debtor's prison into the fresh air and sunshine of solvency and financial sobriety.

When we are just getting by, obsessed with the state of our money, doing a juggling act with our bills and fending off creditors, we are living in survival mode, emotionally as well as financially. There is no time or energy available to expand our horizons, to use our talents, express our creativity, or discover our right livelihood (as Debtors Anonymous refers to what is often called "vocation"). Becoming who we can be, realizing who we are meant to be, is a remote concern when we are living in financial chaos.

Individual Timetables for Recovery

Each newcomer to Debtors Anonymous has his own timetable for recovery. None of us goes at the same pace. It may take some compulsive debtors a few months to experience the fruits of using the tools and taking action steps, and these men and women may achieve financial stability and pay off their debts relatively quickly. Others, in dire straits with collection agencies and with the Internal Revenue Service, may take a number of months, or even a couple of years to arrive at a workable spending plan and debt repayment plan.

But sooner or later, after we have reached a plateau in practicing our program, we will discover that the Steps, principles, and tools operate at levels in our lives we couldn't have imagined. Of course we could not have imagined how the program would change our lives when we were newcomers either. Other recovering debtors may have had a different experience, but in my case, my pressure group worked with me on an ideal spending plan after I had become firmly grounded in using the spending plan we had created from my spending records. After I was out of crisis, had been living within my plan for a number of months, and had implemented stage one of my repayment plan (using only one hundred dollars of my income for creditors, but regularly increasing that amount), my team members suggested we take a look at an ideal spending plan.

Needs Versus Wants

The first action my pressure group members asked me to take was to list ten things I currently needed in my life and then ten things I wanted. Because most compulsive debtors have difficulty distinguishing between needs and wants, this assignment was a helpful prioritization exercise. My current spending plan primarily addressed needs, although it certainly included categories for entertainment, restaurants, and so on, which, in my pre-DA life, I had considered unavailable luxuries (forcing me to charge them, of course). By expanding my thinking about what was possible and achievable, this exercise also prepared me to create an ideal spending plan.

I puzzled over which items belonged on which list, but finally came up with the following:

Needs	Wants
1. New eyeglasses	1. A personal computer
2. A bicycle	2. Massage once a month
3. Health club membership	3. A trip to Disney World with my thirteen-year-old niece
4. A new Yankee birdfeeder	4. New fountain pen
5. Bookshelves for the living room	5. A new wardrobe
6. A new living room lamp	6. A new steam iron
7. A new pair of dress shoes with lower heels	7. Fresh flowers at home and work every week
8. A pair of prescription sunglasses	8. Symphony tickets
9. A food processor	9. A living room couch
10. A new mattress	10. A CD player

My pressure group pointed out that most of the items on my needs list were of two types: personal care and household. Since many compulsive debtors commonly experience deprivation in these two areas, my items were predictable and certainly legitimate needs. The wants list had a variety of items: household, entertainment, sports, aesthetic, nature, and vacation. The personal computer, although appropriate to the wants list at the time, later became a business necessity and thus a need.

Creating categories for these "extra" needs as well as the wants in my current spending plan gave me an even greater sense of flexibility and prosperity than I had previously felt in my spending plan. Even if we allocated only five dollars to start with, we created space in the plan for saving specifically for large items, such as the computer and the couch, and we allocated small amounts immediately for such things as fresh flowers and low-heeled dress shoes.

Moving toward Our Next Level of Life

Then my team members suggested we create an ideal spending plan together, very much as we had created the regular spending plan, but our horizons were to be expanded this time. Whereas the first spending plan provides a set of guidelines for spending in a balanced, conscious way that meets our needs as newly recovered debtors, the ideal spending plan enlarges the plan structure by encouraging us to imagine and dream. What would we eventually like to spend on both needs and wants? If we could create our ideal categories with ideal amounts of money, what would we put into the plan? Whereas the first spending plan begins to shift our paradigm by moving us from lack to plenty, from debting to get what we needed to planned spending to meet those needs; the ideal spending plan provides the structure for us to express in concrete financial terms where we would like to go from here. This plan refines and develops the principles we learned in creating and implementing the first plan. It gives us a financial blueprint for the next level of our lives.

There is something miraculous about putting on paper one's intentions, objectives, visions, and, yes, spending plans. Whether it is a vision for one's life that an individual writes down and then shares at a "visions" DA meeting, or a set of intentions jotted down as guidelines for the next month of work, there is power and energy in shaping and sharing the words. Time and again I have experienced, in my own life and in the stories of other men and women, the reason-defying phenomenon of giving voice to dreams, aspirations, and goals. I have posted intentions on my refrigerator door and looked up one day several months later to discover that most of them have effortlessly come to pass—because in writing them down and making them visible, I made a space for them to occur.

The Ideal Spending Plan

The ideal spending plan operates on the same premise, and, as a DA tool, it not only creates a more spacious financial structure, but it also acts in a metaphorical way to enlarge the arena for us to move toward our life's visions, toward right livelihood, toward claiming, perhaps for the first time, our talents and skills, our creativity. It encourages us to think boldly, dream deeply, and act courageously.

I am grateful that my pressure team members suggested the creation of an ideal spending plan after I had about a year and a half of recovery under my belt. I needed the grounding I had received from consistently using the other, preliminary tools of DA. By the time I drew up my ideal plan, I had been regularly balancing my checkbook to the penny within twenty-four hours of receiving the bank statement, I had paid off thousands of dollars of debt, I had experienced the elasticity and freedom the spending plan gave me, I was providing for myself all the things I really needed, and I no longer lived in reaction to negative surprises. I knew I was ready for a deeper level of DA work. I had had enough experience of miracles being "commonplace in this program," as the Big Book of Alcoholics Anonymous says, to know that the same Higher Power that had supported me in not debting one day at a time could now support me in becoming a larger self, in being who I was meant to be, in using the talents and creativity I had been given.

Taking a look at the ideal spending plan at the end of this chapter (page 189), we see that the total expenses add up to $4,890. An income of at least $60,000 is needed to be able to actually implement this plan. The creator of this ideal plan may choose to put the plan into practice or she may choose to use it as a goad to her imagination, as something to look forward to in the future. At the time this plan was created, my yearly income was $42,500, so an additional $17,500 would have been required if the plan were to be implemented. Just as in the original spending plan, however, the ideal plan provides flexibility, manageability, and choice, all of which have been in short supply previously in debtors' lives.

Dealing with Negativity

The negative, self-debting voices that kept compulsive debtors living from a limited sense of self, rather than from a larger self, do not suddenly disappear forever just because we are working our program. The voices that told us we'd never have enough to meet our needs are the same ones that laugh derisively at the idea that we could actually live from an ideal spending plan—or that we have something unique to give the world as a result of our own talents and creativity, that we could actually make enough money and also enjoy what we're doing to earn it. But by the time we encounter the ideal spending plan and the issues of right livelihood and creativity, we have enough experience, strength, and hope to know that these negative voices aren't powerful enough to defeat the Steps, principles, and tools of our program. We know that the world is bigger than these voices, and we have resources to draw upon.

I love the way Anne Lamott describes her handling of these negative voices in her book *Traveling Mercies: Some Thoughts on Faith*. She has found she can squelch the little monsters that screech at her by imagining them as little mice. She merely grabs each one by the tail and inserts it firmly into a mason jar, covering it with a lid that diminishes the sound. Each of us needs some little imaginary device like Lamott has to put these negative voices in their place. So many of us have focused on these voices that accuse us of worthlessness for so long that we believed that we were incapable of living from anything but a very small self. We had forfeited the possibility of living from a larger self until we found resources larger than we were.

One day my sponsor said to me, "You will find that these negative voices never completely go away, but you will have the resources to deal with them." I was surprised to find myself relieved at what he said. I guess I knew in my heart of hearts that those voices were probably a permanent part of the human condition, and it was helpful to be told the truth—that they'd probably never completely shut up, but I myself would get better at dealing with them. That made sense to me. Nevertheless, these voices had wreaked havoc in my life for a long time; they had set up a loudspeaker system in my brain, drowning out the voices of support and encouragement, the voices that said, "You can do it!"

I'll never forget a humorous—and painful—story told by a regular at my home meeting the first year I was in DA. Kevin said that the noise in his head, the negative, clamoring voices dominating his consciousness, had been so loud for so long that he began wearing a Walkman whenever he possibly could. He would turn up the volume to its highest decibel to drown out the voices. One day he was walking down a busy street and narrowly escaped being run down by an irate motorist who had honked repeatedly at Kevin, who, of course, had been oblivious to the warning. After that, Kevin said, he had gotten worried. He had bought the Walkman to drown out the noise in his head, but now he thought he might be going deaf and all that he would ever be able to hear would be that same noise in his head. Fortunately, Kevin's accusing voices grew weaker as his program grew stronger, and he lost neither his life nor his hearing.

The negative, self-debting voices take a variety of forms. Sometimes they have us compare ourselves to others, and of course we are found wanting. As the program says, we compare our insides to other people's outsides, and we find ourselves on the "short end of the stick." Another way we find ourselves undermined is in our failure to trust our intuitions and perceptions. "That can't be happening; they wouldn't do that," we say, but it is and they are. Our failure to trust what we inwardly know is just another instrument of self-debting.

A particularly virulent form of self-debting shows up in our "shoulds." This way of undermining ourselves is uncannily lethal because it carries parental and societal authority. Shoulds have the stamp of approval, and although they have their place, they are fatal to the development of a larger self, of our visions and our right livelihood, our talents and our creativity. It is often the voice of the shoulds that says, "Who do you think you are that you could have what you want?" This attitude never takes into account that our deepest desires are the ones that spring forth from our deepest selves.

It is these desires that give birth to our creativity and motivate us to develop our talents and gifts.

Ethan, a chronic underearner with many unused talents, could never seem to break out of his low-paying, no-challenge jobs. One night at a DA right livelihood meeting, which focuses on using our talents, skills, and aptitudes to earn a living rather than fitting into the cookie mold merely to make money, Ethan suddenly recalled something his authoritarian father had said to him years before when he remarked that his entry-level job in a large corporation wasn't using any of his innate talents or skills: "You're lucky to have a job, and anyway, somebody has to do that work."

Reclaiming Our Dreams

A particularly powerful DA visions meeting one day evoked powerful memories for a number of men and women who longed to be using more of themselves in their employment situations. A large-framed, middle-aged man found himself in tears as he recalled the dreams he had set aside so many years before. "My family said being an artist was only for sissies and they refused to finance a college education if I majored in art," Jason said.

Fortunately, this middle manager at a nonprofit agency had been offered an early retirement package that made it possible for him to both meet his financial obligations and pursue his artistic leanings, either as a vocation or an avocation. Although Jason felt a great deal of sorrow for his lost dream and his unlived life, he was grateful to be able to reclaim it before it was too late.

Other negative voices that have kept us living from a limited sense of self, as well as from a limited income, are fear, a sense of being overwhelmed, the belief that we have nothing unique to offer, and the conviction that we are not creative or talented. All these attitudes, feelings, and beliefs are forms of self-debting and keep us from having and realizing visions and dreams, goals and objectives, right livelihood and creative talents.

As we clear up our money and our lives by applying the principles and tools of DA to our situations, we start to see how self-debting behaviors, attitudes, and beliefs have operated in deeper levels in our lives than we could possibly have known. The clarity and order in our finances and in our practical, material lives frees us to apply our program to reclaiming our dreams and our creativity. As we share our stories in right livelihood meetings, hearing ourselves describe our work history or employment chronology, we gain a larger perspective on what we've done for a living. Perhaps we've worked only to earn money, and that no longer feels like enough. We don't want to waste any more time at work that doesn't intrinsically hold value and meaning for us. Perhaps, like Jason, we gave in to the parental shoulds in our lives and sold our dreams down the river or put them on hold. Now we find ourselves wanting to reclaim them.

Maybe, like Kevin, an authoritarian voice we internalized long ago is still running our lives. We make do with a ho-hum job because, like true debtors, we think we are lucky to have anything at all and besides, if somebody has to do this job, shouldn't it be me?

As previously mentioned, the road of recovery is not a predictable, linear, sequential road. It is, rather, a spiral, a cyclical journey. Just when we think we've completed our work, the bottom falls out and we discover a whole new level awaits us. The path becomes a series of exciting discoveries, even if we feel fainthearted at the prospect of more hard work.

We thought we came into DA to get out of debt and set our money lives straight. But now we have the opportunity to get out of self-debting behaviors, attitudes, and beliefs and set our creative lives straight. And we can't afford to stand still, to be in stasis, for as the old maxim points out, We cannot stand still without going backward. So if we don't want to lose the recovery we've worked so hard to achieve, we've got to go on. That seems to be the way our Higher Power set it up, to make us keep claiming our gifts and then developing them so we can give them back.

Finding Your True Calling

> The only problem you have is to find your true calling in life. Everything else will fall into place. . . . You will have all the supply that you require to meet your needs, and this means that you will have perfect freedom, for poverty and freedom cannot go together.
>
> —*Anonymous*

A weekly participant in a Debtors Anonymous meeting in the Midwest, Yvonne had been working her program for about three years and had cleaned up her money act. In addition to her weekly home meeting, Yvonne was also attending the once-a-month right livelihood meeting in a neighboring city. As she listened and shared her own story in this meeting, she began to see clearly the beliefs that had held her captive to a particular employment pattern.

Yvonne was awakened one night by a dream that seemed so real she didn't know where she was for a moment. She had dreamed that the house she lived in was physically affixed to the house her boss and his family lived in, which was actually ten miles away. As she watched from the street, a demolition crew completely leveled her house, even destroying the foundation. As Yvonne later said, it didn't take a rocket scientist to decipher the dream code, although she did have a session with her psychotherapist to look closely at the images and figures in the dream and to discuss her associations and feelings. It was clear that Yvonne's sense of value had come from pleasing her boss rather than exercising her own talents, which were considerable. The arrival of the demolition crew signaled the demise of this old, dependent attitude, clearing the way for a new season of autonomy and change.

Yvonne, a capable, well-organized, articulate liberal arts graduate, had made a career of being a highly paid, efficient executive assistant to several powerful chief executive officers of large corporations. Although she was well aware that this career did not use her deepest talents, nor did it provide the sense of autonomy she longed for in her work life, she justified her position by telling herself that it paid well, her bosses respected and needed her, and she was, after all, near the seat of power, where important decisions were made. What more could she want? She would be crazy to give up the salary, the benefits, the pension plan, the sense of affirmation she got from the important men for whom she served as their right hand. A growing feeling of dissatisfaction plagued her, however, and as she became more aware of the beliefs that had governed her career choices, she could no longer hide the pattern from herself. She saw that she had been getting value through the personal approval of men with authority and power. She got to wield influence and authority as adjunct to the CEO, as trusted confidant, as keeper of his time and of his professional and personal confidences. His power washed over her, giving her power through proximity, with none of the accountability or responsibility that belonged only to him.

Although this career would have been perfectly legitimate for someone who really wanted to be an administrative assistant to a CEO, it was the wrong career for Yvonne. She had chosen it for reasons that were illegitimate in her life, and it was preventing her from exercising the autonomy and creativity she deeply desired in a career. Just in case she didn't see the picture clearly, her dream was reinforcing what she was discovering in her right livelihood meeting— that she needed to find her own independent career where her value sprang from her own creative activity rather than from the approval of a powerful CEO who validated her for supporting him. The dream was hopeful, despite the image of demolition, for it showed the foundations of an old, outdated attitude crumbling, preparing Yvonne to live in her own house, a residence that was not dependent upon or affixed to a powerful executive in whose reflected glory she basked.

Today, Yvonne owns her own thriving catering business. Despite the headaches of an entrepreneurial lifestyle, Yvonne loves being her own boss, deciding on her own clientele, using her creativity in menu creation, food preparation, and presentation. She operates her business from her own house, which is not affixed to anyone else's.

Following is my ideal spending plan. Feel free to model your own ideal spending plan on this sample.

Ideal Monthly Spending Plan

Category	Amount
Mortgage	2,000.00
Telephone	100.00
Electric	60.00
Gas	50.00
Food	300.00
Household	100.00
Personal Care	150.00
Fast Food	30.00
Gas/Car	50.00
Entertainment	100.00
Periodicals	20.00
Mail/Stamps	15.00
Business Supplies	30.00
Internet	20.00
Dry Cleaning	20.00
Gifts	100.00
Charity	50.00
Clothing	100.00
Arts/Crafts	40.00
Pets	40.00
CDs, Cassettes, and So On	25.00
Car Maintenance	40.00
Restaurants	100.00
Flowers	50.00
Health Club	50.00
Sports Equipment	25.00
Weekend Excursions	100.00
Recreational Travel	150.00
Gardening/Plants	30.00
Home Furnishings	100.00
Books	25.00
Computer/Home Office	150.00
Vacation Savings	150.00
Savings	300.00
Contingency	200.00
Total Monthly Expenses	4,870.00

Exercises

Set aside about an hour to complete the following exercises. The ideal spending plan should expand your horizons and give you an opportunity to include categories you never dreamed of having. Don't limit yourself; think big!

1. Make a list of ten things that you need and then ten things that you want. Did you have trouble deciding which list each item should belong to? Explain. Were you surprised by anything that showed up on either list?

2. Create an ideal monthly spending plan that would enable you to purchase wants as well as needs. Using the sample provided as a guide, create your categories and then place an ideal sum in each category. What is the total cost of the allocations you have made in this plan? How much greater is the cost of these allocations than your regular spending plan? What categories did you add to this spending plan? Would you have thought of including these categories a year ago? Several months ago?

3. If you could make your living doing anything you wanted, what would your dream job be; that is, what would your right livelihood situation look like? What is prohibiting you from making your living through your right livelihood?

4. Name one step you could take now toward earning your income from your right livelihood.

10

Experiencing Life as a Gift: Cultivating the Capacity to Receive

[Grace] comes to get you where you are
but it doesn't leave you where it found you.
— Anne Lamott, *Traveling Mercies*

"It's not about the money" were the unexpected words I had heard at my first DA meeting. "And if I believe that, you'll tell me another one, right?" I had wanted to say to the small group of recovering debtors who had come over to welcome me and, having heard me describe my desperate plight in the meeting, to offer some encouragement.

Having traveled the road of recovery from compulsive indebtedness for more than seven years now, I can say that what looked like a journey from debt to solvency was indeed that, but it was much, much more. This road proved to be a spiritual pilgrimage that was convened by money but was much larger and deeper than money per se. From where I stand now on this pilgrimage, I can look back and see that my money situation seven years ago was a direct reflection of an inner state.

Creating Space

What I ultimately discovered, as I moved along the spiral of increasing awareness and transformation in the DA program, was that my ability to receive had been so limited and my fear and sense of lack had been so great that I had had no space available to receive all the bounty that the Creator had provided. No matter how much abundance life offered, I could not receive it because my receptors were broken, bent, twisted. So this pilgrimage, although I did not realize it at the time, was not just about getting out of debt; it was also about uncovering my restrictive attitudes and limited beliefs, my inability to depend on my Higher Power as the source of my supply. It was about learning, over time, to clear away the debris that had cluttered my life, prohibiting me from receiving the abundance that is ready and waiting to be experienced.

My journey in DA was a process of discovering that this abundance had been there all along, but my own negative programming had created barriers to my knowing and experiencing this reality. It was as though I had been partially blind all my life and once the negative programming, the old behaviors, attitudes, and beliefs had been peeled away, then a new world appeared. It has been said that spiritual work is really about making ourselves available for receiving the gifts the Creator is so anxious to give us, gifts we sometimes seem loathe to receive. It has also been said that if life is a banquet, most people are starving to death.

I had a dream during my first year in recovery that gave me some perspective on my indebtedness. In the dream I had inherited a set of china that had been in the family for a couple of generations. Although the plates in the set were ample, it became very clear in the dream vignette that the cups were too small, that they simply couldn't hold enough. Although the significance of these images was clear at the time, it took several years of practicing the principles of my program to fully appreciate the levels of meaning contained in the image of the small cups.

An Attitude of Gratitude

A friend of mine recovering from alcohol addiction once said that during her first few months of attendance at Alcoholics Anonymous meetings she heard several people say that they were grateful for their alcoholism because it had put them on a path leading to a rich spiritual life. She had thought at the time that surely these people were insane to make such an observation, but in due course she had arrived at the same conclusion. For me and for everyone I know in Twelve Step fellowships, the anonymous programs are mediators of grace, for they did indeed take us exactly where we were and how we were but did not leave us the way we were. They became the instrument of "unmerited divine assistance," as *Merriam Webster's Collegiate Dictionary* defines *grace*. And the only response to being awakened to the presence of a grace that permeates life is gratitude.

> *It is not happiness that makes gratefulness,*
> *but gratefulness that makes happiness.*

—David Steindl-Rast, *A Listening Heart*

Of all the things that can help us cultivate the capacity to receive, the most essential is what the program calls "an attitude of gratitude." Gratitude increases compassion, enlarges inner space, and short-circuits entitlement and resentment.

It is a mystery to me how the Twelve Step principles seem to effortlessly evoke a sense of gratitude in participants. I see this phenomenon in the lives of recovering debtors and I can feel it in my own. I know how I'm doing by the state of my gratitude. It is a barometer of my spiritual well-being.

The Gift of Life

It is impossible to requisition paradigm shifts as if they were merchandise. Such changes come in their own time, but we can do the footwork and we can create a state of readiness. I will never forget a radical shift that happened to me seemingly out of the blue one day. I had been involved in program work for several years and had also just experienced the loss of a loved one, an event that has the power and potential to open one's heart and to create readiness. It was a rainy Saturday afternoon in April, and I was relaxing with a good book after a hectic work week. I paused for a moment, looking out over my patio into the pine trees beyond. A few chickadees and a cardinal were feasting on black oil sunflower seeds at my feeder.

All of a sudden, in an inexplicable way, a most ordinary moment became extraordinary. I was struck by the realization that Life itself and my Life were pure gifts, that I had been given this precious thing called Life, that it had come from a Source and would return to that Source, and that I had the opportunity to use this Life, on loan from my Source, as best I could. I realized that this Life was an opportunity, that I could do with it what I chose but I was not the author or owner of it; it was a purely temporary arrangement, gratuitously given. I was only a steward in this interlude between where I had come from and where I was going. This realization lasted but a moment, but it re-arranged my entire life. It stood my priorities on their head and opened a window onto a new vista. I had already been experiencing an increasing sense of the plenitude of the universe, but this moment of heightened perception allowed me to experience Life itself as the biggest gift of all.

Recognizing Abundance

In addition to being handed a sense of Life itself as a gift, I began to experience nature as a personal gift from the Creator of the universe. This personal sensibility in no way felt restrictive; that is, I didn't feel it was for me and no one else. Rather, I felt this bounty had been created for everyone, but I was experiencing it for the first time (perhaps since childhood) in a very personal way. I began to do what I called "gratitude writes" after encountering these gifts. One day, back from a walk in the winter rain (something I would have previously abhorred), I wrote:

> *I took a walk in the afternoon rain. The gorgeous winter colors were muted; the oatmeals and sepias and burgundies, and it was all free, and all for me. I have a sense of the bounty of nature in my life in ways I have not had before; this is real abundance.*

I began to notice in meetings how often gratitude surfaced in the things people shared. "I have a gratitude today . . ." someone would say. Others would allude to making a gratitude list, particularly if they were feeling out of kilter. Just writing down the gifts in their lives seemed to shift people from feeling deprived or angry or entitled to feeling enriched and grateful. I adopted the practice and found myself appreciating and being grateful for things I had never noticed before:

heavy, deep, slumbering sleep
the smell of summer rain on hot pavement
the feel of raw silk
the smell of ink in a new book
the graininess of Arrowhead Mills cereal
the beauty of the grain of wood in my grandfather's oak chest
the sound of wind in aspen trees
the light, tinkling, crystal sound of my wind chimes

Somehow this newfound sense of gratitude began to affect my interactions with other people. I had not been pleased to discover, somewhere along the line in the awarenesses evoked by practicing the DA principles, that I was not always as magnanimous as I had thought toward others. If someone else did well, it might mean that I did less well. I did not take pleasure in admitting that I didn't always wish the best for others. But in the universe I was discovering, one in which amplitude is the rule and is personally bestowed on creatures by the Creator, generosity of spirit could flourish; more for someone else did not equate to less for me. Such a shift began to cultivate a greater sense of abundance in relationships. It seemed there might be no end to the benefits to be reaped from having sowed interior generosity. I recalled a verse from the Old Testament I had memorized as a child, seeing it with new eyes: "See if I will not open the windows of heaven and rain down blessings upon you, more than you need" (Malachi 3:10).

Exercises

The following exercises may take some time to fully complete. However, they are all exercises that can be started today.

1. Create a gratitude list, enumerating whatever comes to mind that you feel grateful for. Your list might include material possessions, relationships, your work, your talents, your experience of nature, and intangible values like faith, courage, loyalty, and so on.

2. Make it a point to express your gratitude to others. As an experiment, for a period of one week thank one person each day for some kindness she has done or express your gratitude for a characteristic she has that touches you in a special way. At the end of the week, write a one-page reflection on what happened, for you and for the others, as a result of your expressions of gratitude.

3. Each day, starting today, jot down in a notebook five things you are grateful for. Keep up this practice for one month. At the end of the month, read through your gratitude list. Has this practice made you more aware of all the gifts in your life? Comment.

Appendixes

Appendix A

The Twelve Steps of Alcoholics Anonymous*

1. We admitted we were powerless over alcohol—that our lives had become unmanageable.
2. Came to believe that a Power greater than ourselves could restore us to sanity.
3. Made a decision to turn our will and our lives over to the care of God *as we understood Him.*
4. Made a searching and fearless moral inventory of ourselves.
5. Admitted to God, to ourselves, and to another human being the exact nature of our wrongs.
6. Were entirely ready to have God remove all these defects of character.
7. Humbly asked Him to remove our shortcomings.
8. Made a list of all persons we had harmed, and became willing to make amends to them all.
9. Made direct amends to such people wherever possible, except when to do so would injure them or others.
10. Continued to take personal inventory and when we were wrong promptly admitted it.
11. Sought through prayer and meditation to improve our conscious contact with God *as we understood Him,* praying only for knowledge of His will for us and the power to carry that out.
12. Having had a spiritual awakening as the result of these steps, we tried to carry this message to alcoholics, and to practice these principles in all our affairs.

---

* The Twelve Steps of AA are taken from *Alcoholics Anonymous,* 3d ed., published by AA World Services, Inc., New York, N.Y., 59-60. Reprinted with permission of AA World Services, Inc. (See editor's note on copyright page.)

Appendix B

The Twelve Steps of Debtors Anonymous*

1. We admitted we were powerless over debt—that our lives had become unmanageable.

2. Came to believe that a Power greater than ourselves could restore us to sanity.

3. Made a decision to turn our will and our lives over to the care of God as we understood Him.

4. Made a searching and fearless moral inventory of ourselves.

5. Admitted to God, to ourselves, and to another human being the exact nature of our wrongs.

6. Were entirely ready to have God remove all these defects of character.

7. Humbly asked Him to remove our shortcomings.

8. Made a list of all persons we had harmed and became willing to make amends to them all.

9. Made direct amends to such people wherever possible, except when to do so would injure them or others.

10. Continued to take personal inventory and when we were wrong promptly admitted it.

11. Sought through prayer and meditation to improve our conscious contact with God as we understood Him praying only for knowledge of His will for us and the power to carry that out.

12. Having had a spiritual awakening as the result of these steps, we tried to carry this message to compulsive debtors, and to practice these principles in all our affairs.

---

*Reprinted with permission of Debtors Anonymous. Adapted from the Twelve Steps of Alcoholics Anonymous with permission of Alcoholics Anonymous World Services, Inc. (AAWS), New York, N.Y. (See editor's note on copyright page.)

Appendix C

The Twelve Traditions of Alcoholics Anonymous*

1. Our common welfare should come first; personal recovery depends upon A.A. unity.

2. For our group purpose there is but one ultimate authority—a loving God as He may express Himself in our group conscience. Our leaders are but trusted servants; they do not govern.

3. The only requirement for A.A. membership is a desire to stop drinking.

4. Each group should be autonomous except in matters affecting other groups or A.A. as a whole.

5. Each group has but one primary purpose—to carry its message to the alcoholic who still suffers.

6. An A.A. group ought never endorse, finance, or lend the A.A. name to any related facility or outside enterprise, lest problems of money, property, and prestige divert us from our primary purpose.

7. Every A.A. group ought to be fully self-supporting, declining outside contributions.

8. Alcoholics Anonymous should remain forever nonprofessional, but our service centers may employ special workers.

9. A.A., as such, ought never be organized; but we may create service boards or committees directly responsible to those they serve.

10. Alcoholics Anonymous has no opinion on outside issues; hence the A.A. name ought never be drawn into public controversy.

---

* The Twelve Traditions of AA are taken from *Twelve Steps and Twelve Traditions*, published by A.A. World Services, Inc., New York, N.Y., 129-87. Reprinted with permission of AA World Services, Inc. (See editor's note on copyright page.)

11. Our public relations policy is based on attraction rather than promotion; we need always maintain personal anonymity at the level of press, radio, and films.

12. Anonymity is the spiritual foundation of all our traditions, ever reminding us to place principles before personalities.

Appendix D

The Twelve Traditions of Debtors Anonymous[*]

1. Our common welfare should come first; personal recovery depends upon D.A. unity.
2. For our group purpose there is but one ultimate authority— a loving God as He may express Himself in our group conscience. Our leaders are but trusted servants; they do not govern.
3. The only requirement for D.A. membership is a desire to stop incurring unsecured debt.
4. Each group should be autonomous except in matters affecting other groups or D.A. as a whole.
5. Each group has but one primary purpose—to carry its message to the debtor who still suffers.
6. A D.A. group ought never endorse, finance, or lend the D.A. name to any related facility or outside enterprise, lest problems of money, property, and prestige divert us from our primary purpose.
7. Every D.A. group ought to be fully self-supporting, declining outside contributions.
8. Debtors Anonymous should remain forever nonprofessional, but our service centers may employ special workers.
9. D.A., as such, ought never be organized; but we may create service boards or committees directly responsible to those they serve.
10. Debtors Anonymous has no opinion on outside issues; hence the D.A. name ought never be drawn into public controversy.

---

[*] Reprinted with the permission of Debtors Anonymous. Adapted from the Twelve Traditions of Alcoholics Anonymous with permission of Alcoholics Anonymous World Services, Inc. (AAWS), New York, N.Y. (See editor's note on copyright page.)

11. Our public relations policy is based on attraction rather than promotion; we need always maintain personal anonymity at the level of press, radio, and films.
12. Anonymity is the spiritual foundation of all our traditions, ever reminding us to place principles before personalities.

Appendix E

Debtors Anonymous Preamble*

Debtors Anonymous is a fellowship of men and women who share their experience, strength and hope with each other that they may solve their common problem and help others recover from compulsive debting. The only requirement for membership is a desire to stop incurring unsecured debt. There are no dues or fees for D.A. membership; we are self-supporting through our own contributions. D.A. is not allied with any sect, denomination, politics, organization or institution; does not wish to engage in any controversy; neither endorses nor opposes any causes. Our primary purpose is to stay solvent and help other compulsive debtors achieve solvency.

---

* Reprinted with the permission of Debtors Anonymous. (See editor's note on copyright page.)

Index

HAZELDEN INFORMATION AND EDUCATIONAL SERVICES is a division of the Hazelden Foundation, a not-for-profit organization. Since 1949, Hazelden has been a leader in promoting the dignity and treatment of people afflicted with the disease of chemical dependency.

The mission of the foundation is to improve the quality of life for individuals, families, and communities by providing a national continuum of information, education, and recovery services that are widely accessible; to advance the field through research and training; and to improve our quality and effectiveness through continuous improvement and innovation.

Stemming from that, the mission of this division is to provide quality information and support to people wherever they may be in their personal journey—from education and early intervention, through treatment and recovery, to personal and spiritual growth.

Although our treatment programs do not necessarily use everything Hazelden publishes, our bibliotherapeutic materials support our mission and the Twelve Step philosophy upon which it is based. We encourage your comments and feedback.

The headquarters of the Hazelden Foundation is in Center City, Minnesota. Additional treatment facilities are located in Chicago, Illinois; New York, New York; Plymouth, Minnesota; St. Paul, Minnesota; and West Palm Beach, Florida. At these sites, we provide a continuum of care for men and women of all ages. Our Plymouth facility is designed specifically for youth and families.

For more information on Hazelden, please call **1-800-257-7800**. Or you may access our World Wide Web site on the Internet at **www.hazelden.org.**